"There are always alternatives to war, as the voices in this book testify. Let us listen to their voices of wisdom, and start to disarm our mindsets, talk to our enemies and solve our problems in a civilized way. We all know in today's highly militarized and dangerous world, this nonviolent path to peace makes sense."

— **MAIREAD CORRIGAN MAGUIRE**
NOBEL PEACE LAUREATE

"Fifty years ago, President Eisenhower expressed his concern about the 'campaign of hatred' against us in the Arab world, for reasons that his administration knew were sound. By now, particularly during the Bush years, fear and often hatred of the US have spread widely and deepened. Even Europeans now rank the US as the greatest threat to world peace, far above China, Russia, Iran or North Korea. Americans should be deeply concerned about these developments, and the reasons for them. The questions raised in these essays are the pertinent ones, and the answers developed should be pondered carefully by those who are concerned with their country and given its immense power—the entire world and future generations."

— **NOAM CHOMSKY**

"*American Wars: Illusions and Realities* sets the record straight. War is not peace, only peace is peace. If the Iraq War is a teachable moment about the real nature of U.S. aggressive intentions in the world, then this book should be in the core curriculum."

— **AMERICAN FRIENDS SERVICE COMMITTEE**

"In 1960, US General Thomas Power declared: 'The whole idea is to kill the bastards! At the end of the war, if there are two Americans and one Russian, we win!' We have to make sure that US foreign policy is not run by people with the mentality, the heart, and the soul of a General Power. That type has occupied the White House all too frequently, as *American Wars* shows us."

— **WILLIAM BLUM, author of *Rogue State***

AMERICAN WARS: ILLUSIONS AND REALITIES

AMERICAN WARS

ILLUSIONS
AND REALITIES

edited by

PAUL BUCHHEIT

CLARITY PRESS, INC.

© 2008 Clarity Press, Inc.

ISBN: 0-932863-56-6
   978-0-932863-56-0

In-house editor: Diana G. Collier

Library of Congress Cataloging-in-Publication Data
American wars : illusions and realities / edited by Paul Buchheit.
   p. cm.
  Includes bibliographical references and index.
  ISBN-13: 978-0-932863-56-0
  ISBN-10: 0-932863-56-6
1. United States—Military policy—Moral and ethical aspects. 2. War—
Moral and ethical aspects—United States. 3. National characteristics,
American. 4. Values—United States. 5. Self-deception—Political
aspects. 6. United States—Foreign relations—Philosophy. 7. Mass
media and war—United States. I. Buchheit, Paul.
  UA23.A6632 2008
  172'.420973—dc22
                              2008000512

Clarity Press, Inc.
Ste. 469, 3277 Roswell Rd. NE
Atlanta, GA. 30305
USA
http://www.claritypress.com

TABLE OF CONTENTS

ACKNOWLEDGMENTS

American Wars: Illusions and Realities is the product of the efforts of many people who have lived through war and have studied about war, who understand its devastating effects on its innocent victims, and who wish to clear up the many misconceptions about war that cause us to keep fighting.

I have learned something from every contributor to this book. I have benefited from the excellent books and articles and websites that provided information missing from the mainstream media.

I am indebted to the educators and students at Chicago City Colleges, DePaul, University of Illinois, and University of Chicago who helped to promote awareness of the issues through our global initiative.

I have discovered, most of all, that while an understanding of the truth about war comes only with a good degree of effort, the satisfaction derived from that knowledge is enough to sustain enthusiasm for further learning. And I truly believe that an understanding of the truth will inspire Americans to work toward improving their country.

— **Paul Buchheit**

INTRODUCTION

American Wars vs. American Values

On this page and the next are two pictures dramatically addressing the plight of children in wars. The first picture (above) shows an American soldier tenderly holding a little Iraqi girl. As stated in the caption, she appears to be "glad he's there."

On the following page, a second picture shows a little girl, maybe seven years old, with a horribly damaged foot and shrapnel marks on her face. She is being cradled in the arms of a man, perhaps her father or grandfather. Her hand is outstretched, as if she were reaching out to a friend when a bomb exploded at their feet.

AP/Wide World Photo

The first photograph is an illusion. The child, according to photographer Damir Sagolj, had just been injured in an attack in which her mother was killed and her father "riddled with bullets." An artist from Iowa Presidential Watch doctored the photo and presented it to the American media to show how "our soldier tenderly holds an Iraqi child in his arms."[1]

The second photograph shows the true image of a little girl who was the victim of the March, 2003 US/UK coalition attack on the Iraqi city of Basra. It provides clear evidence of the horrific nature of wars—but few such images find their way into the mass media, any more than do images of wounded, shattered and dead American soldiers.

I look again at the second picture and imagine, for a moment, that this is my daughter. A sickening tightness forms in my stomach, and I force the thought out of my mind. What if this were to happen in America? The media, and people everywhere in our country, would grieve for a little girl that is so much a part of us. They would be outraged by the loss of an innocent life.

But this happened in Iraq, not America. We see little of this type of thing in America, so it is easy for us to keep the madness of war out of our minds.

We need to learn more about the realities of war.

Americans believe that technology has changed the nature of modern war, thereby upholding our country's noble principles by allowing us to fight with less killing and less pain, both to our troops and to the citizens of the countries where we fight. We are certain that we are fighting for *honorable* purposes, to promote peace and democracy. That elected officials, military leaders, and media owners are generally *truthful* about our country's activities. That we are sufficiently *aware* of war's impact on our own lives. That modern warfare shows *compassion* for the innocent people in the countries we oppose. That our wars reflect a type of *altruism* toward the world, as we seek economic progress and environmental sustainability for all. And, finally, that we have a *realistic* sense of war's inevitability as a part of the human condition.

The purpose of this book is to present the truth about these many illusions. We Americans hold dear the values of honor and truth and compassion. We feel self-assured about our role in the world, and we are realistic about the world's response. These values are presented by our leaders as reasons to fight our wars: our quest for democracy is honorable, and certain to help other nations, even though the short-term path to success may necessitate a period of intense suffering. But perhaps we are fooling ourselves. The rest of the world tells us we are wrong, and that they fear our government more than any other. We may be unaware of the truth, or indifferent, or too absorbed by our daily lives to take the time to understand the bigger picture, as sketched by the world for our benefit. That is the purpose of this book—to show how illusions about war are distorting our own cherished values, and making it more important than ever to learn about war's sobering reality.

American Wars: Illusions and Realities is divided into six sections, each of which examines one of our highly regarded human values. Within each section specific illusions associated with the value will be viewed in terms of the facts and images and observations that we genuinely recognize as reality.

The contributors to the book are human rights activists, academic scholars, veterans, and experienced researchers, all of whom are troubled by the false illusions of war and wish to report the truth. Their viewpoints on these sensitive issues will encourage us to look at the big picture, to reflect upon information rarely offered by the mainstream media, to analyze it for ourselves. And their words will remind us that the little Basra girl in the second picture had the same hopes and dreams as children in our own country until the violent adult world intervened.

Kriss Russell

HONOR

We Fight for the Right Reasons

We Americans believe that our wars are just. We believe we have intervened in Central America to safeguard our shores from the threat of communism, and we station our troops within the borders of our allies to secure them against our common enemies. The romanticized image at the left reflects the vision of America and its troops held by many.

We feel it's a matter of honor to advance democracy in Iraq, the land of mankind's earliest civilization, where a brutal dictator tortured and killed his own people. We wish to offer our way of life to those who would share our moral and economic ideals. Our young men and women are not dying in vain, for they are defending America's honor, and through their efforts we will bring peace and prosperity to the people of the world.

But what will happen to our society when we come to realize that much of this is not true? What will happen when Americans start to learn the true picture about our government's wars, and the true motives behind their glowing pretexts?

Will we resist, and demand that our actions match our proclaimed intentions, and thereby seek to restore the honor we have lost in the eyes of the world, and then in our own?

Or will we simply ignore the reality, persisting in an illusion that continues to erode our cherished values?

[1]

ILLUSION
We fight for peace and democracy.

REALITY

**American wars are fought to defend or extend
US corporate, financial or political interests,
often contrary to the interests of the countries where we fight.**

Paul Buchheit

"The war in Iraq is really about peace."
— George Bush, visiting wounded troops on April 11, 2003

Americans believe we fight our wars to maintain peace and promote democracy. We believe in these values, and our government and media assure us they are upholding them in our name. We feel confident that America is built on good moral standards of fairness and justice. Naturally, we wish to extend these values to the world.

Yet the United States has a long history of occupying other people's territories.[1] It has been our 'manifest destiny' to tell others how to live. George Washington, writing to Lafayette about the Iroquois Indians in 1779, said he would like to "extirpate them from the country." The Native Americans referred to Washington as the 'town destroyer.' [2] Manifest Destiny as a formal policy has its roots in the Monroe Doctrine, which provided precedent for U.S. expansion on the American continent.[3]

Teddy Roosevelt used the Monroe Doctrine to justify intervention in Latin America. In 1901 Woodrow Wilson wrote, "Our interest must march forward, altruists though we are; other nations must see to it that they stand off, and do not seek to stay us."[4] President Taft declared in 1912: "The whole (western) hemisphere will be ours in fact as, by virtue of our superiority of race, it already is ours morally."[5]

In more politically correct times, discretion is employed, but the sentiment hasn't changed. The focus since WW2 has been on oil. In 1945, the U.S. State Department described Saudi Arabia as "a stupendous source of strategic power, and one of the greatest material prizes in world history."[6] The 'Carter Doctrine' asserts that anyone else's attempt to control the Persian Gulf would be "an assault on the vital interests of the United States," and would be "repelled by any means necessary, including military force."[7] A 1992 Pentagon statement declared "In the Middle East and Southwest Asia, our overall objective is to remain the predominant outside power in the region and preserve U.S. and Western access to the region's oil." And, ironically, from the same report: "It remains fundamentally important to prevent a hegemon or alignment of powers from dominating the region."[8]

A Brief History of Recent American Interventions

The United States has experienced only 20 years since 1789 in which its military has not been active somewhere in the world.[9] In addition to our War of 1812, Mexican-American War, Civil War, Spanish-American War, World War 1, World War 2, Korean War, Vietnam War, Persian Gulf War, and Iraqi War, we have militarily intervened in other countries over 130 times since the start of our country, with the majority of interventions occurring since World War 2.[10]

In 1953 the United States helped Great Britain to overthrow Iranian leader Mohammad Mossadegh, a charismatic and learned man who was democracy-minded, nationalistic, and supported by 95 percent of his people. He attempted to take the oil industry back from Great Britain, which paid the Middle East country less than 16% of the profits for its own oil. Members of the Eisenhower administration spent large amounts of money to bribe the Iranian news media to foment fear and distrust of Mossadegh's government among his country's citizens. The campaign was orchestrated by Kermit Roosevelt, grandson of Theodore Roosevelt, who ran the CIA Operation Ajax. They hired thugs to attack respected members of society, and to claim allegiance to Mossadegh while looting the city. Members of Parliament and protestors were bribed to speak out against him. Newspaper editors called him an atheist, an imperialist, and a traitor. The plan worked remarkably well, for in just a few days there was a call for his resignation, and in the end the oil was flowing once again to the western world.[11]

In 1950 Jacobo Arbenz was democratically elected president of Guatemala. He tried to help native Mayan Indians regain rightful ownership of their land, which had been appropriated by the United Fruit Company (UFC). But the powerful conservative base in the U.S. saw the land reforms as communist activities, and by late 1953 the CIA was excitedly planning the bribes, propaganda, infiltration, and sabotage that would harass Arbenz into a humiliating resignation. In the forty years following, an estimated 200,000 Guatemalans, most of them native Mayans, were slaughtered in one of the most brutal ethnic cleansings in recent history. A Guatemalan

Historical Commission concluded in 1999 that US-trained and US-supported military forces had been responsible for most of the human rights abuses during the war. President Clinton admitted U.S. involvement and issued a formal apology.[12]

In 1962 Juan Bosch became the Dominican Republic's first democratically elected president in 40 years. He introduced land reform, low-rent housing, nationalization of businesses, and public works projects. As a proponent of civil liberties, he promised that Communists would not be prosecuted. Nationalization and civil liberties, and especially Bosch's tolerance of communists, frightened Washington, and the media picked up on it. A *Miami News* article with purported CIA links said "Communist penetration of the Dominican Republic is progressing with incredible speed and efficiency." Bosch was forced out in 1963 by a military coup supported by the United States. *Newsweek* magazine said, "Democracy was being saved from communism by getting rid of democracy."[13]

In 1970 Salvadore Allende was elected President of Chile. The South American country had a strong democratic society with a high literacy rate and bright prospects for its sizable middle class. Allende was a passionate supporter of people's rights and the nationalization of industries that were controlled by American companies. In 1973 he was assassinated (or pressured into committing suicide) during an assault on the Chilean parliament led by General Augusto Pinochet, whose CIA-supported coup led to the torture and murder of thousands of people over the next two decades.[14]

In the 1980s in Angola, in the name of anti-communism, Presidents Reagan and George H. W. Bush and the apartheid government of South Africa supported the UNITA guerrillas in their 20-year civil war, calling their leader Jonas Savimbi a 'freedom fighter.' But Unita conducted a reign of terror. They killed hundreds of thousands of people in an act of ethnic cleansing paralleling the scenes in Somalia, Liberia, and Sudan. Young boys were tortured and killed, and the women were burned at the stake, while the director of the savagery regularly visited the White House.[15]

In 1984 the Sandinista government of Nicaragua, which had won a free election with 2/3 of the vote, managed a wide range of public services, provided free education and health care, and launched a literacy campaign that reduced the illiteracy rate from over 50% to less than 20%. The World Health Organization called Nicaragua a "model country in health care." The anti-communist Reagan administration supported the Contra rebels against the Sandinistas. Reagan called the rebels his 'freedom fighters.' The U.S. began mining Nicaraguan harbors, and the World Court found the United States guilty of "unlawful use of force" and international terrorism.[16]

In 1990 Jean-Bertrand Aristide, a Catholic priest, was elected president in Haiti's first free democratic election. He was popular among the poor for his social programs, and he opposed industry privatization measures that primarily benefited the upper class. After Aristide was twice overthrown by a US-backed military coup, the country was spending most of its foreign reserves to pay off its debt to the United States, even as the U.S. withheld foreign aid. Conditions in Haiti remain desperate today, with crumbling roads and infrastructure and nonexistent public services. Haiti is the poorest country in the western hemisphere, with unemployment at 70% and half the adults illiterate. The great majority (85%) of Haitians live on less than $1 U.S. per day. The richest one percent of the population controls nearly half of all of Haiti's wealth.[17]

In 2002 George Bush and Tony Blair met to discuss plans to remove Saddam Hussein from power, based on beliefs about weapons of mass destruction and a connection to Al Qaeda, both of which later proved false. Evidence from the meeting showed that air strikes began in 2002 without Congressional approval, and that attempts were made to provoke Saddam into a retaliatory strike that would justify war. According to British foreign intelligence agent Richard Dearlove, "the intelligence and facts were being fixed around the policy" (of removing Saddam).[18] In fact, the State Department's Future of Iraq project indicates that planning for regime change had already begun in 2001.

The belief persists in this country that the spread of American morals and culture will eventually bring a prosperous peace to everyone. But comprehensive studies have revealed the opposite, especially when military interventions are counted as periods of conflict.[19] *The Economist* ranked the U.S. 96th out of 119 countries in its Global Peace Index of the most peaceful countries in the world.[20] Although the Human Security Report 2005 found that the number of armed conflicts has decreased around the world since the end of the Cold War in 1991, the U.S. has actually been involved in *more* wars, on the average, since before the end of the Cold War.[21] Each year we spend an increasing amount on the materials of war. We are the world's leading weapons trader. We preside over a world ruptured by economic inequality. And to ensure our continued success, even in the face of suspected connections between occupation and terrorism, we keep a quarter of a million U.S. troops in 135 countries around the globe.[22]

Peace through War

Far from being a peace-loving society, we are in fact a military-oriented society. The U.S. is responsible for almost half of the world's total military expenditures, which surpassed $1.1 trillion in 2005.[23] President Bush approved a record U.S. defense budget for 2008 — more than $480 billion. This will be augmented by an additional $145 billion for the wars in

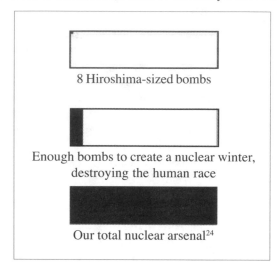

8 Hiroshima-sized bombs

Enough bombs to create a nuclear winter,
destroying the human race

Our total nuclear arsenal[24]

Iraq and Afghanistan.[25] The Congressional Research Service (CRS) puts the total estimated cost of the Iraqi and Afghanistan conflicts at $811 billion, much more than the $549 billion spent on the Vietnam War.[26]

The 2008 budget increases spending on aircraft, submarines, and weapons designed to counter a single powerful enemy, rather than scattered clandestine guerrilla or terrorist forces.[27] In an effort to curb our reliance on military responses to world affairs, a task force of 14 military and foreign policy experts published "A Unified Security Budget for the United States 2006," which recommends cutting $53 billion from the military budget and spending $40 billion more on international affairs, counter-terrorism, and peacekeeping operations.[28] The waste and inefficiency in U.S. military spending is also highlighted by a Natural Resources Defense Council (NRDC) report that describes "an excessive stockpile of high-yield Cold War weapons that now clearly are no longer needed."[29]

This is taxpayer money that could have been used for health and education programs for American citizens.

There is a concern that our extravagant military spending encourages other nations to compete with us. China is rapidly increasing its defense spending, although its annual total is only about 1/10 of that in the United States.[30] In Russia, it is estimated that military expenditures have tripled since the year 2000.[31] President Putin remarked that, like the U.S., Russia would not be denied access to regions of the world essential to its survival. In 2004 Russian Defense Minister Sergei Ivanov explained that their newly developed advanced WMDs were a response to U.S. escalation. Vladimir Putin recently said, "It wasn't us who initiated a new round of arms race...We have pulled out all our heavy weapons from the

European part of Russia…and cut our military by 300,000 men. And what about our partners? They are filling Eastern Europe with new weapons…What we are supposed to do? We can't just sit back and look at that."[32]

Arms for Everyone

According to the U.S. Congressional Research Service, the U.S. has sold over twice as much weaponry as any other country. *Nearly half of the arms deliveries to developing countries* in 2005 came from the United States.[33]

In 2003, 20 of the top 25 recipients of U.S. arms sales in the developing world were declared *undemocratic or human rights abusers* by the U.S. State Department's own Human Rights Report. These included Saudi Arabia, Egypt, Kuwait, the United Arab Emirates, and Uzbekistan.[34]

The United States sold weapons to 18 of the 25 countries *involved in active conflicts* in 2003.[35]

The U.S. *armed both sides* in conflicts between India and Pakistan, Iran and Iraq, Greece and Turkey, Saudi Arabia and Israel, Peru and Ecuador, China and Taiwan, and Israel and the rest of the Middle East.[36] In Saudi Arabia, the U.S. helped to protect the monarchy from other Saudis who were also using arms supplied by the U.S.[37]

Despite U.S. prohibitions against arms sales to 'rogue' nations in Africa, South America, Asia, and the Middle East, weapons continue to enter these countries from other countries that are supplied by the United States.[38] In Iraq, weapons intended for government forces often end up in the hands of militants and organized gangs.[39]

Democratization and Peace

Do our attempts to democratize the world lead to peace? It is generally true that democracies do not fight each other. But democracies do not necessarily react peaceably to other forms of government. A comprehensive study by political scientists Jack Snyder and Edward Mansfield showed that over the past 200 years *developing* democracies went to war much more frequently than stable autocracies or established democracies."[40]

Other studies recommend against installing democracies in countries with a large ethnic divide.[41] Based on these conclusions, it would seem unwise to try to force democratization on a nation in any hurried way—even if it could be concluded that "forcing democracy" was an otherwise workable notion.

But our motives in the quest for a democratic world are suspect.

The U.S. has regularly supported dictatorships in the past, and today supports undemocratic regimes in Saudi Arabia, Egypt, and Pakistan, to name just a few. Its pro-democracy image in the Middle East may have been irretrievably harmed, not just by its effort to depose the democratically elected Hamas government in Palestine, but by its continued reference to Hezbollah, which is a regular participant in Lebanese elections and in fact heads government ministries, as a terrorist organization.[42]

A March 2004 Pew Research Report found that America's credibility overseas had been damaged by the Iraqi War. Majorities in France and Germany believed that U.S. incentives are control of oil and world domination.[43] Recent (2007) polls by BBC World Service and the Pew Research Center show how the global view of U.S. involvement has continued to deteriorate.[44] Opinions of the U.S. have soured not only in Middle Eastern countries but also among traditional allies such as Germany, France, and Britain.[45] Perhaps most disturbingly, polls are beginning to indicate that anti-Americanism is being directed not only at the U.S. government, but increasingly at the American people.[46] Other nations apparently can't understand why we, as determined advocates of democracy, don't rein in our aggressive government, and they suspect that we either support the combative behavior of our leaders or simply don't care.

The Profit Motive

If not for peace and democracy, why else do we fight wars? Presidents use war to inspire nationwide feelings of patriotism and to improve their public opinion ratings. John F. Kennedy's ratings rose to 83% after the Bay of Pigs incursion into Cuba. The invasion of the little island of Grenada bolstered Ronald Reagan's poll numbers. President George H. W. Bush enjoyed an 89% favorable rating during Desert Storm. When George Bush declared war against Iraq in March, 2003 his ratings went from 53% to 68%.[47]

And then there is the profit motive. In the words of Major General Smedley Butler, "War is a racket." Butler was a World War 1 veteran who at the time of his death was the most decorated Marine in U.S. history. He served our country during the beginnings of imperialist expansion under McKinley and Teddy Roosevelt, and he observed the growth of big business and the suppression of labor in World War 1. An excerpt from his book:

> In the World War a mere handful garnered the profits of the conflict. At least 21,000 new millionaires and billionaires were made in the United States during the World War ... How many

of these war millionaires shouldered a rifle? How many of them dug a trench? How many of them knew what it meant to go hungry in a rat-infested dug-out? How many of them spent sleepless, frightened nights, ducking shells and shrapnel and machine gun bullets? How many of them parried a bayonet thrust of an enemy? How many of them were wounded or killed in battle?[48]

War profiteering in the U.S. occurred long before World War 1, and it still occurs today. In 1778 George Washington said: "There is such a thirst for gain [among military suppliers]...that it is enough to make one curse their own Species, for possessing so little virtue and patriotism." A different message was sent in World War 2, when many business executives were 'dollar-a-year' men who donated their services to the war effort. Franklin D. Roosevelt and Harry Truman considered war profits immoral. But after the war Dwight Eisenhower recognized the ominous merging of corporate and military interests: "We must guard against the acquisition of unwarranted influence, whether sought or unsought, by the military-industrial complex."

At the start of the Iraq War in 2003, at least nine members of the Defense Policy Board, which advises the Pentagon, had ties to companies with $76 billion in defense contracts.[49] A Department of Defense organizational chart called 'Civil Administration of Postwar Iraq' contained 16 boxes, each with name and responsibility. None of them were Iraqis.[50]

Executive Excess 2006[51] reported on its study of 34 publicly traded U.S. defense contractors and found that *average annual* CEO pay doubled from $3.6 million to $7.2 million since the War on Terror started. This parallels the massive defense spending increases by the U.S. military. Stock prices for these companies increased 50% between 2000 and 2005, even as the S&P 500 dropped 5% over the same time period.

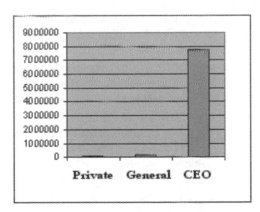

Figure 1: Pay in Dollars (from Executive Excess 2006)

Just 34 CEOs have pocketed $1 billion in four years, enough to pay the yearly salaries of a million Iraqis. Many unemployed Iraqis have joined the ranks of the insurgents that we're fighting today. CEO pay for defense contractors grew about 50% faster than military pay between 2001 and 2005. Figure 1 shows the 2005 pay for an army private, a general with 20 years experience, and a defense contractor CEO.

Halliburton, Dick Cheney's former company, is the most notorious war profiteer, with over half the Pentagon contracts for war services. Halliburton's revenue in 2006 was $22.5 billion, three times its revenue from 2004. The company's stock price is approximately three times higher than in 2004. As noted by halliburtonwatch.org, the number of American dead is also three times the number in 2004.[52]

The Presidential team has played a significant role in Halliburton's rise.[53] As Secretary of Defense, Dick Cheney commissioned a study recommending the company for a lead role in military support operations around the world. Two years later he became CEO of Halliburton. Soon after that he became Vice President. President Bush signed an executive order in 2003 granting oil industry companies such as Halliburton immunity against lawsuits over environmental disasters and human rights violations.[54]

According to reports by CorpWatch and Congressman Henry Waxman, Halliburton has been implicated in overcharging, unsubstantiated charges, poor workmanship, and safety problems.[55] The company decided in early 2007 to move its corporate headquarters to Dubai, a well-known tax haven in the United Arab Emirates.[56] In addition to the tax savings, Halliburton stands to benefit from the greater difficulty in prosecuting a foreign-based company.

Bechtel is another war-profiteering company. In the 1980s, as Saddam Hussein was dropping thousands of chemical bombs on his own people, Bechtel and its friends in the Reagan Administration were working with the Iraqi government to build an oil pipeline. In 2006 the Special Inspector General for Iraq Reconstruction (SIGIR) found that the Basra Children's Hospital proposed by Bechtel for $50 million was a year and a half behind schedule and $90 million over budget. Because of the gross mismanagement, the contract was canceled. SIGIR also found that most of Bechtel's water and electricity projects are incomplete or malfunctioning. The Bechtel Group admitted that not a single one of its 40 water plants is being operated properly, and they blamed the Iraqis for the problems.[57]

It's not only about Halliburton and Bechtel, though.[58] The five main defense contractors — Lockheed Martin, Boeing, Raytheon, Northrop Grumman, and General Dynamics — took $35 billion of our tax dollars in 2006 to produce major weapons systems that target Cold-War-era enemies and do little to fight terrorism.[59] The five arms companies are all among the *top seven* federal contractors for 2007.[60] Both the companies and their foreign customers benefit: Israel spends much of its $1.8 billion in annual military aid from the U.S. to buy Lockheed's F-16 jet fighters from Lockheed.[61] But U.S. citizens make the payments.

The Pentagon sometimes sells its newest military equipment, necessitating the development of even better weapons to maintain an advantage over the countries that are buying from us.[62]

Vice Admiral Jack Shanahan, a NATO Commander, said in 2001: "As long as we continue to sell our best aircraft, we've got to go out and invent something even better. Eventually, we're going to have to fight them."[63] The Pentagon's 2000 budget sought to replace the F-15, 'the world's most advanced aircraft,' with Lockheed and Boeing's F-22, 'the world's most advanced aircraft.' Each plane cost four times as much as the plane it was replacing.[64]

Lockheed's F-35 Joint Strike Fighter is the latest example of a flawed and super-expensive war machine. Its development at a total cost of $260 billion makes it the most expensive weapons program ever.[65] According to the Center for Defense Information, its design makes it "inherently too fast to find targets on the ground independently, too limited in 'fuel fraction' and weapons payload to persist on the battlefield, and too thin skinned and delicate to survive tactical air defenses typical on the conventional battlefield."[66] Yet despite the fact that the F-35 is not ready for combat, two of them are included in the $99.7 billion emergency supplemental appropriations request in 2007 for the wars in Afghanistan and Iraq.[67] And, in an ominous revisiting of Admiral Shanahan's words about selling our best aircraft, we've arranged to sell 100 F-35s to Turkey, which already has over 200 F-16 fighter planes, is 94th on the United Nations' Human Development Index, and has a 9% favorable view of the U.S. among its citizens.[68]

Finally, the Bush family itself has lucrative ties to the war.[69] Neil Bush, the President's brother, was paid an annual salary to "help companies secure contracts in Iraq." Former President George H. W. Bush helped the Carlyle Group secure billions of dollars in defense contracts after 9/11. Brothers Marvin and Jeb and Uncle William (Bucky) all have defense-related deals with military contractors.

Conclusion

Over and above the power-seeking and the profit-making, can we achieve peace and democracy in a world increasingly threatened by terrorism? A comprehensive study using the highly regarded MIPT-RAND terrorism database[70] shows a sevenfold increase in the annual rate of fatal terrorist attacks around the world since the March 2003 invasion of Iraq.[71] Almost half of all violent civilian deaths after the initial invasion occurred in the just-ended fourth year of the war, with the deadliest bombings occurring in August 2007.[72]

A University of Chicago study of 71 terrorists concluded that suicide attackers are motivated more than anything else by their aversion to foreign occupation.[73].

The same motives were expressed in a 2007 NBC interview of jailed Iraqis who had attacked American forces.[74] An assessment by 16 U.S. intelligence agencies, including the CIA, the FBI, the State Dept., and all four branches of the armed forces, revealed that the occupation of Iraq has contributed to an increase in the overall terrorist threat.[75]

The consensus of 100 foreign policy experts is that the highest priority in the war on terrorism should be a reduction in our oil dependency.[76] We have yet to learn that in the pursuit of peace and democracy there are alternatives to fighting.

Further Reading

Bacevich, Andrew J. *The New American Militarism.* Oxford University Press, 2005.
Barash, David P. and Webel, Charles P. *Peace and Conflict Studies.* Sage Publications, 2002.
Butler, Smedley. *War is a Racket.* Round Table Press, 1935.
Chomsky, Noam. *Hegemony or Survival.* Henry Holt & Co., 2003-2004.
Chua, Amy. *World on Fire.* Anchor Books, 2004.
Denson, John V. "War and American Freedom." In Denson, John V. (Editor). *The Costs of War: America's Pyrrhic Victories.* Transaction Publishers, 1997.
Goodman, Amy. *The Exception to the Rulers.* Hyperion Books, 2004.
Hedges, Chris. *What Every Person Should Know About WAR.* Free Press, 2003
Kinzer, Stephen. *Overthrow: America's Century of Regime Change from Hawaii to Iraq.* Henry Holt & Co., 2006.
Petras, James. *Rulers and Ruled in the US Empire.* Clarity Press, 2007.
Roy, Arundhati. *An Ordinary Person's Guide to Empire.* South End Press, 2004.
Solomon, Norman. *War Made Easy.* John Wiley & Sons, 2005.
Zakaria, Fareed. *The Future of Freedom.* W W Norton & Co, 2004.
Zinn, Howard. *The Zinn Reader.* Seven Stories Press, 1997.

2

ILLUSION
We fight to defend our personal freedoms.

REALITY

**War provides governments with a reason
to restrict any manifestation of opposition to their policies.**

Judi Nitsch

"All those who seek to destroy the liberties of a
democratic nation ought to know that war is the
surest and shortest means to accomplish it."
— Alexis de Tocqueville

"Once a government is committed to the principle of
silencing the voice of opposition, it has only one way
to go, and that is down the path of increasingly
repressive measures, until it becomes a source of
terror to all its citizens and creates a country where
everyone lives in fear."
— Harry S. Truman

"You have the right to free speech…
as long as you're not actually dumb enough to try it."
—The Clash, "Know Your Rights"

After some cajoling, I convinced two friends to attend an
emergency antiwar rally in Times Square on Thursday, March 20, 2003 —
a day marked by emergency protests and the official start of the Iraq war.
I was no stranger to antiwar protests. Weeks ago, Indiana University
students successfully organized a student walkout and antiwar rally — a
protest coordinated among universities and high schools across the
country in the "Books Not Bombs" day of action. Such work introduced
me to bureaucratic permit mazes for rally space, a march path, amplified

As convoys of National Guard reinforcements finally rolled into New Orleans, Louisiana Governor Kathleen Blanco clearly indicated they were not there to bring succor to Americans, but rather to protect property. "These troops are battle-tested. They have M-16s and are locked and loaded," she said. "These troops know how to shoot and kill and I expect they will."

sound, and a host of seemingly accessible liberties. New York City, though, was a new and frightening experience, as its 'guardians' had perfected the physical and bureaucratic stifling of protest.

The New York Police Department (NYPD) had tested the repressive post 9/11 waters by impeding a massive peace march a month earlier, in February 2003. Despite early submissions of permit requests and protest plans, the march organizers, United for Peace and Justice (UFPJ), received a response for the NYPD only after the New York Civil Liberties Union (NYCLU) intervened. Using stall tactics and permit denials, the City attempted to squash the march with all its bureaucratic weight, including what Chief Esposito claimed was "an informal policy in the fall of 2002 of denying parade permits for all protest marches in midtown Manhattan."[1] A District Court ruled in favor of the City's decision to deny a march near the United Nations for "pos[ing] unacceptable security risks" and found a total ban on protest marches "reasonable." Vague "security concerns" trumped civil liberties, as members of UFPJ settled for a stationary protest in Midtown Manhattan.

Now, in March, spurred on by a gray evening drizzle, my friends and I headed to Times Square and into the signs of infrastructural intervention — but we were not yet literate in NYPD counter-protest tactics. Many of the subway stations near and the one opening directly into Times Square were suddenly inaccessible, forcing us to creatively navigate the subway system and walk many blocks to reach Time Square. Upon our arrival, NYPD ushered us into metal pens along the sidewalk. More bodies filled our pen as the hours passed, and no word came explaining their use. Through the cages, we watched the military spectacle of "Operation Atlas," the NYPD's code-named counter-protest operation launched that day, rumble around us. Individual armed units patrolled Manhattan avenues, and streets and clusters of riot-geared police graced every subway stop we passed through. Helicopters slowly flew over the crowds, casting a panoptic spot over us. Heavily-armed police directed us to the pen entrance that their colleagues guarded. Intimidated, my friends and I headed to the entrance and convinced the stone-faced cop that we were harmless tourists who had wandered inadvertently into the protest. Rolling his eyes, he waved us through the gate, thereby ending our introduction to New York State's common modes of counter-dissent.

Mainstream media accounts of the March 20th emergency protest in Times Square told a different and decidedly vague story of the evening's events. Only one Associated Press story reported on any of the emergency A.N.S.W.E.R (Act Now to Stop War and End Racism) protests, counting "hundreds" of participants at an afternoon mobilization and speculating sparse attendance at the rush-hour event I attended.[2] Only *The Village Voice* recorded "thousands" at the evening protest.[3]

The writers at Fairness and Accuracy in Reporting (FAIR) have led the struggle for accurate crowd counts in media analysis of antiwar protests from the war's beginning. Inaccurate police counts supplant the counts of independent organizations that mainstream media outlets could but refuse to employ. Indeed, FAIR organized a massive media campaign to demand accurate antiwar coverage from the *New York Times* and National Public Radio, as both misrepresented participation in a sizable antiwar march in Washington, D.C. in October of 2002, which both "organizers and police suggested was likely Washington's largest since the Vietnam era", according to the *Los Angeles Times*.[4] After receiving over a thousand letters from media activists, the outlets issued neither a second report on the antiwar movement nor an apologetic correction to the 'mistake.' Size, protestors argue, does matter, and the repeated undercounting suggests a concerted downplaying of domestic resistance to the war.[5]

Of course, the numbers game is played only by those media outlets that choose to cover the U.S. antiwar movement at all. As early as the summer of 2003, media analysts Steve Rendall and Tara Broughel analyzed mainstream media coverage of the Iraq war, and their discoveries were alarming:

> Nearly two thirds of all sources, 64 percent, were pro-war, while 71 percent of U.S. guests favored the war. Antiwar voices were 10 percent of all sources, but just 6 percent of non-Iraqi sources and 3 percent of U.S. sources. Thus viewers were more than six times as likely to see a pro-war source as one who was antiwar; with U.S. guests alone, the ratio increased to 25 to 1.[6]

Stacking the deck, media outlets typically filled pundit spots with current and former government employees, often those from the Department of Defense.[7] Despite the larger numbers of dissenting citizens, mainstream media outlets preferred "official" voices to independent critics or grassroots activists, relegating opposition to a meager 3 percent of its total coverage.[8] Popular Sunday news shows or mainstream evening news programs presented an imaginary national consensus on the war.[9] The activist perspective, antiwar or otherwise, is often reduced to soundbites from nameless individuals responding to on the street interviews, rather than from the articulate and informed representatives of sizable organizations like A.N.S.W.E.R. and United for Peace and Justice.[10]

Boston Herald, Angela Rowings

Boston police arrest members of Veterans for Peace for disrupting a 2007 Veterans Day ceremony at City Hall Plaza. The veterans were arrested when they protested their exclusion from a Veterans Day event by refusing to move away from the podium.

In their three-week study, Rendall and Broughel could not identify one show that involved an extended interview with an individual holding an antiwar perspective.

While the major media steadily ignore antiwar activists, the federal government has taken a strong interest in them. The Patriot Act handed considerable power to the federal government and its investigatory agencies to survey and discipline its dissenting citizens. So-called "counterterrorism measures" spawned costly programs that involved increased surveillance on civilians and created, according to the American Civil Liberties Union (ACLU), "a chilling of protest."[11] As I witnessed on March 20, 2003, New York City comfortably slipped into police-state garb labeled "national security." Operation Atlas, with its initial price tag of $5 million a week, extended police power to survey domestic political groups.[12] The plan's architect, Police Commissioner Raymond Kelly, drew on his previous work in the CIA to justify the need for domestic surveillance in his 'terrorism preparedness' program, as he rewarded officers with generous overtime pay to police poor neighborhoods and write parking tickets.[13]

The 2003 rallies demonstrated how controlling the citizenry through surveillance is justified by terming it a 'national security' measure. A week before the Iraq war's start, the *Associated Press* reported a federal judge lifting an 18-year-old limitation on NYPD's surveillance of political groups.[14] "Protection" becomes synonymous with "surveillance," even in situations of peaceful dissent. A recent ACLU report details Department of Defense (DoD) files on peaceful protest groups gathered through a reporting mechanism known as Threat and Local Observation Notices ("TALON"). From Vietnam veterans to college students to Quakers, the groups under government surveillance are depicted as engaging in the "subversive" activities of disrupting ROTC recruitment, holding candlelight vigils, and chanting outside of military bases. The reports labeled the groups as non-threatening and yet the DoD kept the information, as well as personal data on protestors.[15]

The ACLU report, among other documents detailing government surveillance of lawful dissenters and government data mining projects, makes a strong case for counter-vigilance against government trampling of those civil rights vital to a healthy democracy at home as the government pursues its efforts to "bring" democracy to Iraq and Afghanistan.[16] These reports also amplify an eerie echo of dark moments in U.S. history: mass deportations during WWI, the internment of Japanese-Americans during WWII, the "communist" witch-hunts of the 1950s, the unlawful surveillance of civil rights activists, amongst others. History teaches us how readily our government will exploit wartime powers to arrest dissention and how vital our dissent is in arresting government policy antipathetic to true American values.

Further Reading

Chomsky, Noam. *Rogue States: The Rule of Force in World Affairs*. Cambridge: South End Press, 2000.

Churchill, Ward & Jim Vander Wall. *The COINTELPRO Papers*. Cambridge: South End Press, 2002.

Churchill, War & Jim Vander Wall. *Agents of Repression: The FBI's Secret Wars Against the American Indian Movement and the Black Panther Party*. Cambridge: South End Press, 2002.

Enloe, Cynthia. *Maneuvers: The International Politics of Militarizing Women's Lives*. Berkeley, Los Angeles and London: University of California Press, 2000.

Enloe, Cynthia. *Bananas, Beaches and Bases: Making Feminist Sense of International Politics*. University of California Press, 1997.

Enloe, Cynthia. *Does Khaki Become You? The Militarization of Women's Lives*. London, Pandora Press; San Francisco, Harper/Collins, 1988.

Gelderloos, Peter. *How Nonviolence Protects the State*. Cambridge: South End Press, 2007.

Roy, Arundhati. *An Ordinary Person's Guide to Empire*. Cambridge: South End Press, 2004.

Williams, Kristian. *Our Enemies in Blue: Police and Power in America*. Revised Edition. Cambridge: South End Press, 2007.

"President Bush got the world's attention this fall when he warned that a nuclear-armed Iran might lead to World War III. But his stark warning came at least a month or two after he had first been told about fresh indications that Iran had actually halted its nuclear weapons program." ("A Blow to Bush's Tehran Policy" by Peter Baker and Robin Wright, *Washington Post*, Tuesday, December 4, 2007.)

TRUTHFULNESS

We Can Believe Our Decision-Makers

We put our faith in our political leaders, whom we have elected to work for the greater good of the general public. We expect them to keep us properly informed about their activities as public officials. Of course there will be times when we disagree with their decisions, or when actions that seem unnecessary or immoral, such as intervention into another nation's affairs, have a long-term justification that may not be immediately apparent. And at times we will feel a healthy skepticism for the political process in general. But we the people run the show. These are our representatives, and if they fail to tell us the truth they will be replaced, for we trust in democracy.

Our relationship with government is especially significant in times of war. The realities of war exist, for most of us, in a netherworld of brutality that is beyond our willingness or capacity to comprehend. We must depend on our elected officials to speak the truth, our military to take care of our sons and daughters, and our news media to tell us what we need to know. We trust in our leaders to heed the words of Thomas Jefferson: "There is not a truth existing which I fear... or would wish unknown to the whole world."

But what happens when this is not the case— when Americans feel that their president is lying to them, that politicians and military leaders deceive the people they serve, and that the major media cannot be counted on to tell the truth?

Is lying, then, in some insidious manner, to become acceptable within our society as a way of conducting our affairs, because that is what our leaders and opinion-makers do? How can we teach our own children not to cheat in school when everyone knows the president lies? How can we protect our communities from exploitation by public figures who deceive the public trust by promoting their own private agendas?

What are the long-term costs to the fabric of our society when ordinary people realize that our relationship with the world is based on such deception?

3

ILLUSION

Our government tells us the truth about our wars.

REALITY

Our government has lied to us about every one of our wars.

Cindy Sheehan

In other parts of the world, I find a healthy skepticism towards government. I feel that one should not explicitly trust one's government in any affair. Governments lie with facility and regularity, but the one thing they lie about the most is war. When it comes to such grave matters as leading our nation into war and the propaganda surrounding it, we citizens should be the most untrusting and skeptical, but it is often in this very area that we are the most credulous.

Especially in my country, America, one is made to feel unpatriotic or unsupportive of our young men and women in uniform if we object to the reasons for which our leadership is foisting yet another war upon us. And many people who protest adamantly against war stop their protest as soon as the first bomb drops, because they feel they must avoid the appearance of giving "aid and comfort" to the enemy, or undermining our nation's war efforts, or, heaven forbid, not supporting the "troops."

Being a US History major and a citizen of this country, I am only going to concentrate on the lies that have spurred our country into war after war. However, speaking about our entry into the two abominable world wars of last century will necessitate speaking about the European lies that eventually sucked the US down the drain of mass murder, mostly against the will of the American people.

Like many nations before and after us (what I am saying is that we are not unique in our history), our nation was founded on killing, to the extent of the almost complete genocide of the native population. While English settlers were exterminating aboriginal populations in our northeast, Spaniards were doing it in the southeast and west. If a native tribe or population wasn't completely killed off, their way of life was forced to undergo a massive paradigm shift and their communities were

37

forced onto mostly non-arable land with little or no game to hunt. When the first European settler stepped the first white, Christian foot on this continent, there were an estimated 3 million Native Americans. By the end of the 19th century, after that number had been reduced by epidemics of European disease and murder, some tribes had been reduced by 90-95%.

The lies that encouraged the butchering of entire groups of diverse tribes and language groups, with sophisticated societies all revolving around families and a gentle use of resources and land, were numerous. The biggest lie that led to the indigenous extermination was that "Indians" were sub-human, animals, or savages. Such demonization of entire populations has been used repeatedly in the history of the USA to enable our leaders to enslave or slaughter people who range from slightly different to substantially different from Anglo-Saxon or Anglo-Saxonized Europeans, i.e., "Americans."[1]

This demonization of others is quite extraordinary when one thinks of it. What is a national American identity and who is allowed to define who is different from that identity? From the first settlers, we have been religiously and economically diverse and have spoken a wide range of languages. Is a different population one that doesn't speak English? One that is a different color than "white" or one that is not Christian? In WWII, we were fighting two countries whose peoples were mostly white and Christian (Germany/Italy), but for years, with the knowledge of our government, Germany was allowed to commit a mass genocide of European Jews.

One of the very earliest lies that led to war was in the 1846-48 Mexican-American war.[2] President James Polk claimed that Mexicans had killed Americans on "American soil." A young Congressman from Illinois called for Polk's impeachment every day in his famous "Spot" resolutions,[3] demanding that the President give material proof of his lies. As in most cases, Lincoln was a lone voice calling out in the wilderness to try to prevent more carnage. Ironically, as with current members of Congress, once war was officially declared, Lincoln voted for every monetary appropriation—and went on to become the President responsible for killing more Americans than any other.

The US War Between the States can be debated forever, and has been, as to whether that war was a "good war." While people in the South believed that states were sovereign and that the Federal government was usurping too much power, they were also defending an inhumane institution. Many abolitionists in the North worked for decades to abolish black slavery, but the war was not fought to "free slaves." Lincoln's famous "Emancipation Proclamation" was not proclaimed until early 1863 and did not free one slave. As a matter of fact, in a foreshadowing of events to come, President Lincoln suspended habeas corpus and imprisoned war dissenters. The lie that served as a pretext to justify the deaths of almost 700,000 sons of America was that the war was being fought to "free slaves," and this lie has persisted for generations.

Looking back in history, one of the most blatant falsehoods leading to war—and also to our still infant American imperialism—was the lie that got us into the Spanish-American war. This war included one of the earliest uses of the press to foment public outrage, which allowed hundreds of thousands of Philippines to be exterminated, and permanent bases in Cuba and the Philippines to be established and maintained ever since. In 1898, the American battleship, The Maine, exploded in Havana Harbor, and the "yellow" newspapers of William Randolph Hearst trumpeted the fact that Spain blew her up and the war began. It reminds one of Fox News whipping their viewers into a frenzy about al-Qaeda in Iraq (As an aside: a 2003 poll showed that 67% of Fox News viewers still believe that Iraq had links to al-Qaeda, whereas only 16% of PBS/NPR viewers/listeners believe the same thing.[4]). No one really knows why The Maine exploded, but it could have been a boiler, or a "false flag" attack by Americans to start the war. As the questions remain about the 31st President's war record in WWII, Teddy Roosevelt's so-called "taking" of San Juan Hill (which is really not much more than a grassy knoll in Santiago, Cuba) is highly suspect also.

The "war to end all wars" began on lies and continued on lies. America had an isolationist attitude and did not want to enter the European conflict: Americans, that is. The bankers and elitists were chomping at the bit to get a piece of the war profiteering pie and it has been argued that the sinking of the Lusitania was another "false flag" operation to lead America, once again, to the heartbreak of unnecessary war. After WWI, Major General Smedley Butler wrote *War is a Racket*[5], which exposed the immoral and obscene profiteering of war. Another product of WW1 was one of America's greatest novels, Dalton Trumbo's *Johnny Got his Gun.*[6]

The Versailles Treaty, which left Germany off of the "peace" table, led to WWII. Germany was suppressed and oppressed by the treaty that imposed great economic hardship on its civilian society. This allowed a charismatic but evil Adolf Hitler to rise to power. In our xenophobia and political ignorance here in the USA, we tend to overlook the fact that the very same bankers and corporatists that were cheerleaders for American involvement in the first "great" war went on to support Hitler.

Still, after WWI, Americans were in no mood for more carnage. No mothers who had lost brothers and fathers in WWI were ready for their sons to be slaughtered for imperialistic corporate greed, and so the country was not supportive of another war—until Pearl Harbor.[7] There is evidence that the government knew about the Japanese operation before it occurred and did nothing to stop it.

      At issue is American foreknowledge of Japanese military plans to attack Hawaii by a submarine and carrier force 59 years ago. There are two questions at the top of the foreknowledge list: (1) whether President Franklin D. Roosevelt and his top military chieftains provoked Japan into an "overt act of war" directed at Hawaii, and (2) whether Japan's military plans were obtained in advance by the United States but concealed from the Hawaiian military commanders, Admiral Husband E. Kimmel and Lieutenant General Walter Short so they would not interfere with the overt act.

      The latter question was answered in the affirmative on October 30, 2000, when President Bill Clinton signed into law, with the support of a bipartisan Congress, the National Defense Authorization Act. Amidst its omnibus provisions, the Act reverses the findings of nine previous Pearl Harbor investigations and finds that both Kimmel and Short were denied crucial military intelligence that tracked the Japanese forces toward Hawaii and obtained by the Roosevelt Administration in the weeks before the attack.

      Congress was specific in its finding against the 1941 White House: Kimmel and Short were cut off from the intelligence pipeline that located Japanese forces advancing on Hawaii. Then, after the successful Japanese raid, both commanders were relieved of their commands, blamed for failing to ward off the attack, and demoted in rank.[8]

      Pearl Harbor rallied the country to war. Americans like Jeannette Rankin, a Congresswoman from Montana who was the only Congress Rep to vote "nay" on the WWII war resolution, and Charles Lindbergh, who was a pacifist and adamantly opposed to entering WWII, were considered traitorous. Lindbergh was forced out of the country and Ms. Rankin was almost torn apart by an angry mob after her vote.

      The Korean War is a complete mystery to me. After five decades America still has a very strong military presence in South Korea and there is no treaty in place. I visited South Korea in 2006, and the lie that remains is that North Korea is part of the "Axis of Evil" and must be contained. Koreans want unification so they can be reunited with their families. I asked thousands of Koreans who they considered a bigger threat to the stability of their country and region: George Bush or Kim Jong Il…. one hundred percent of them said: George Bush.

All one has to say about our mistake in Vietnam is 'Gulf of Tonkin.'[9] There is little debate about the "rightness" or "wrongness" of that war. Most Americans realize Vietnam was a waste of millions of human lives and almost destroyed our country politically and socially. The great lie that persists about Vietnam is that we "lost" and we can never let that happen again. The way that we can "win" is for the American people to not lose their "will" to fight, and for them to allow the civilian and military leaders all the necessary latitude to wage such wars with little or no protest. After the First Gulf War, which was a "successful" war, President George H.W. Bush said that we had finally broken free of the "Vietnam Syndrome." To him, what counted was not the vastly disproportionate number of Iraqi civilians being killed, or displaced, or sickened and deformed by depleted uranium, but rather that America "won."

The George W. Bush Administration has taken lying about war and propagandizing for war to new heights. During the Bush regime, we are constantly lied to about the reasons for the continuing occupation of Iraq.

First, we were told that Saddam had WMD, and he could deliver those to the USA at any moment. Then we were told that he had connections to al-Qaeda. When those two rationales fail, we are told that we are spreading "freedom and democracy" to the Middle East while our freedoms have been eroded here in the "homeland" and our democracy has been tainted by questionable elections.

From the genocide of our own native population to the genocide of the people of Iraq, the carnage continues with the tacit approval of the American public, who seem to like, or at least accept, being lied to by succeeding administrations.

The only way for these abominable wars to end is for we the people of the United States of America to wake up and realize that being hyper-sensitive to the loss of human life and to the resultant human tragedy of war is more important than being hyper-patriotic and giving our leaders blank checks to wage wars based on lies.

They have *all* been based on lies.

My son, Casey, merely joined a long line of American soldiers who have been killed for lies and corporate greed for all the power and the money.

I am afraid that if we do not wake up and stop it, Casey and his comrades killed in Iraq will just be a drop in the bucket of these continuing wars.

God help us.

Further Reading

Butler, Smedley. *War is a Racket*. Round Table Press, 1935.

Chomsky, Noam. *Hegemony or Survival*. Henry Holt & Co., 2003-2004.

Johnson, Chalmers. Nemesis: *The Last Days of the American Republic*. Metropolitan Books, 2007.

Mihesuah, Devon. *American Indians: Stereotypes and Realities*. Clarity Press, 1996.

Perkins, John. *Confessions of an Economic Hitman*. Plume, 2005.

Sheehan, Cindy. *Peace Mom: A Mother's Journey through Heartache to Activism*. Atria, 2006.

Trumbo, Dalton. *Johnny Got His Gun*. Bantam Books, 1938.

4

ILLUSION
We stay in Iraq to prevent further bloodshed among Iraqis.

REALITY
We disregard Iraqi peace plans and foment inter-ethnic strife as a pretext for ongoing occupation.

Joshua Holland and Raed Jarrar

> *I sent American troops to Iraq to make its people free,*
> *not to make them American.*
> *Iraqis will write their own history, and find their own way.*
> — Remarks by the President on Iraq and the War on Terror,
> United States Army War College, May 2004

Iraq's resistance groups have offered a series of peace plans that might put an end to the country's sectarian violence, but they've been ignored by the U.S.-led coalition.

In May 2007, a majority of Iraqi lawmakers demanded a timetable for U.S. and other foreign troops to leave their country.[1] The very next day, the Al Fadhila party, a Shi'ite party considered moderate by the (often arbitrary) standards of the commercial media, held a press conference, in which it offered a 23-point plan for stabilizing Iraq.

An online search shows that the peace plan was largely ignored by the Western commercial media.

That's par for the course. While every nuance of every spending bill that passes the U.S. Congress is analyzed in minute detail, the Iraqis — remember them? — have proposed a series of comprehensive peace deals that might unite the country's ethnic and sectarian groups and result in an outcome American officials of all stripes say they want to achieve: a stable, self-governing Iraq that is strong enough to keep groups like al Qaeda from establishing training camps and other infrastructure within its borders.

Al Fadhila's peace plan was not the first one offered by Iraqi actors, nor the first to be ignored by the Anglo-American Coalition. Comprehensive plans have been offered by the Ba'ath party, which ruled Iraq for three generations, the Islamic Army in Iraq and other major armed resistance groups and coalitions. The plans vary on a number of points, but all of them shared a few items in common: the occupation forces must recognize them as legitimate resistance groups and negotiate with them, and the United States must agree to set a timetable for a complete withdrawal from Iraq.

Last year, a comprehensive, 28-point proposal for stabilizing Iraq was offered by the nascent Iraqi government itself after long meetings with different Iraqi groups. According to local polls and political leaders, most Iraqis believed it was the proverbial light at the end of the tunnel — the plan was attractive to the vast majority of the public, even those Iraqis affiliated with violent resistance groups. But the plan wasn't acceptable to Washington, and was watered down so as to be unrecognizable under U.S. pressure.[2]

These plans are unacceptable to the Coalition because they (a) affirm the legitimacy of Iraq's armed resistance groups and acknowledge that the U.S.-led coalition is, in fact, an occupying army, and (b) return Iraq to the Iraqis, which means no permanent bases, no oil law that gives foreign firms super-sweet deals and no radical restructuring of the Iraqi economy. U.S. lawmakers have been and continue to be faced with a choice between Iraqi stability and American Empire, and continue to choose the latter, even as the results of those choices are splashed in bloody Technicolor across our TV screens every evening.

While the commercial press focuses on the bloody scenes created by those who have taken up arms against the occupation and the fledgling Iraqi government, the reality is that a significant opposition has been expressed by nonviolent means such as regular demonstrations on the streets of Baghdad and other cities, petitions signed by Iraqis, strikes organized by Iraqi unions, parliamentarians working to create binding legislation, and opinion articles in the dozens of Iraqi newspapers that have proliferated since the invasion. This nonviolent demonstration of Iraqis' anti-occupation sentiment reflects large majorities of all of Iraq's major ethnic and sectarian groups — more than eight out of 10, according to many polls.[3]

As early as 2005, the University of Michigan's Juan Cole reported that the Sadrist movement—named after the father of the nationalist cleric Muqtada al-Sadr—had gathered a million signatures on a petition demanding a timetable for occupation forces to withdraw.[4] More recently, the Arabic press reported that as many as a million Iraqis—a million Shia and Sunni working together—had protested the continuing occupation in Najaf on the fourth anniversary of the fall of Baghdad last month.

Much of the violence in Iraq has been fueled by this systematic disregard for nonviolent means of opposing the occupation. Before they sink down the memory hole, let's recall what just a few of the headlines from the very early days of the occupation were saying:

> "U.S. Soldiers Kill 13 at Iraq Protest Rally"
> Hospital Reports. Associated Press, 29 April 2003.

> "At Least 10 Dead as U.S. Soldiers Fire on School
> Protest"*Independent* (U.K.), 30 April 2003.

> "Two More Die During Protest at U.S. Killings"
> *Guardian*, 1 May 2003

> "More Protesters Fall to U.S. Guns in Falluja;
> Commander Says Americans Will Remain"
> Associated Press, 1 May 2003.

Nonviolent resistance in Iraq continues to be met with violence today. Iraqi nationalists have faced repeated attacks by both Coalition forces and Iraqi separatists—from the bombing of the National Dialogue Front's headquarters in Baghdad to attacks by Shia separatists like SCIRI on Sadr loyalists. At the same time, U.S. officials have heaped praise on —and the White House has feted—Iraqi separatists while dismissing Iraq's nationalists as "extremists" or members of "anti-government forces."[5]

Washington's choice is clear: It can continue to refuse to offer a timetable for leaving, continue supporting Iraq separatists and pro-Iranian groups and push a disastrous oil law that will tear the country apart, or it can return the country to the Iraqis and let them try to put their country back together. Continuing to ignore Iraqis' nonviolent resistance to the U.S. occupation can achieve nothing other than pushing the country towards more violence.

Further Reading

Nakash, Yitzhak. *The Shi'is of Iraq*. Princeton University Press, 2003.
Hiro, Dilip. *Iraq: in The Eye of the Storm*. Thunder's Mouth Press, 2002.
Hiro, Dilip. *Neighbors, Not Friends: Iraq and Iran after the Gulf Wars*. Routledge, 2001.
Shatzmiller, Maya, Editor. *Nationalism and Minority Identities in Islamic Societies*. McGill-Queen's University Press, 2005.

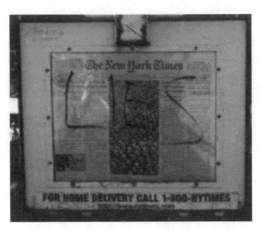

On May 26, 2004, in an Editors Note titled "*The Times and Iraq*", *The New York Times* apologized for its coverage of the lead-up to the war on Iraq. It examined its coverage of the issue of Iraq's weapons and possible Iraqi connections to international terrorists, and found "a number of instances of coverage that was not as rigorous as it should have been. In some cases, information that was controversial then, and seems questionable now, was insufficiently qualified or allowed to stand unchallenged."

As Amy Goodman, author of *The Exception to the Rulers*, pointed out, "It's outrageous to have a simple editor's note buried on page A10, while their repetition of the administrations' lies was consistently given top billing on the front pages of the paper."

In fact, it often went like this: On September 8, 2002, *The New York Times* reported that, according to Bush administration officials, Iraq had "embarked on a worldwide hunt for materials to make an atomic bomb." Dick Cheney went on national TV the same day and referred to *The Times* story as if he were simply reporting the news. In May of 2004, over a year and a half later, *The Times* acknowledged that its story "should have been presented more cautiously."

"Too little, too late," Megan Boler responded in "N.Y. Times Apology Rings Hollow" in the *Toronto Sun*. "Too many people dead.... *The N.Y. Times* and dozens of other media underreported the millions of anti-war protesters in the U.S. and internationally who took to the streets month after month to oppose this invasion."

5

ILLUSION

The mainstream media gives us balanced reporting.

REALITY

**The mainstream media is controlled by a few large corporations
who have conflicts of interest when it comes to war.**

Anup Shah

It is well accepted that a mainstream media, free from governmental control, is paramount for maintaining a functioning, free, and democratic society where the citizenry can make informed decisions and hold those in power to account. The Founding Fathers recognized this in the nation's beginnings, granting the media special protections under the First Amendment. However, in recent decades critical thinking, typically encouraged in schools and public discourse, has slowly given way to blind conformance.[1] For example, just a few months after September 11, Dan Rather of *CBS* admitted that the US media has generally been cowed by patriotic fever. Fear of being accused of lack of patriotism has "kept journalists from asking the toughest of the tough questions."[2] Even into 2007, "questioning power, especially at a time of war, can be perceived as unpatriotic or unsupportive of America's fighting troops."[3]

The Role of Mainstream/Corporate Media

By the end of 2006, a handful of media companies dominated the US media: Disney, AOL-Time Warner (owners of CNN), Viacom, General Electric (owners of NBC), and Robert Murdoch's News Corp. (owners of Fox). Yahoo, Microsoft and Google were three new big players,[4] also global multinationals owning many outlets around the world, and contributing to a global concentration of ownership in the field of communications.[5]

A corporate press itself is not necessarily the problem; the real concern is the *concentration* in media ownership that leads to a narrow spectrum of political and social ideas, and pressure for outlets to fall in line with the owner's interests.[6]

This is what the Federal Communications Commission (FCC) has discovered but does not want to admit. The FCC has long pushed for deregulating media to allow for further consolidation, claiming it will not have an adverse impact on diversity and local coverage. Instead, it has had the opposite effect—so much so that the FCC attempted to destroy its own report confirming this, and in another case suppressed its own findings that the Telecommunications Act of 1996 had resulted in a drastic decline in radio station owners while the number of commercial stations increased.[7]

Commercial-military Interests Influence U.S. Media and Communications Networks

What this also means is that such media outlets are less likely to run in-depth critique or analysis of issues that may reflect negatively on their owners' interests. For example, General Electric is one of the largest military contractors, and Westinghouse, another military contractor, used to own CBS. (Westinghouse has now merged with CBS into the CBS Corporation). Such interests mean the public is less likely to get in-depth analysis that questions excessive military spending, foreign policy critical of US actions, etc.

More generally, these companies have an immense interest in the current neoliberal form of globalization, which is recognized as being related to military dominance, even if this linkage is not often discussed in depth by the mainstream:

> Defense Secretary William Cohen, in remarks to reporters prior to his speech at Microsoft Corporation in Seattle, put it this way, "[T]he prosperity that companies like Microsoft now enjoy could not occur without having the strong military that we have."[8]

The use of the military to pursue economic advantage overseas is not a modern phenomenon; it has occurred throughout history.[9] During European imperialism and colonialism, for example, "gunboat diplomacy" was often employed by Britain and others to gain access to resources and to pry open foreign markets when their domestic markets were saturated. The ideas of the *Project for a New American Century* to use military power to directly consolidate, even extend, American world dominance has resonated strongly with the Bush Administration.[10]

It is in this context that a conformist media comes into being, which nourishes only the appearance of balance and debate. As foreign policy critic Noam Chomsky noted over a decade ago:

The smart way to keep people passive and obedient is to
strictly limit the spectrum of acceptable opinion, but allow
very lively debate within that spectrum—even encourage
the more critical and dissident views. That gives people
the sense that there's free thinking going on…[11]

Fake News (Spin Masquerading as News)

Media consolidation has resulted in reduced staff and diversity
of views.[12] News is increasingly "prepackaged" by public relations firms
and government agencies to make up the deficit.[13]

A great deal of fake and prepackaged news created by US
government departments, such as the Pentagon and the State Department,
has been disseminated through the mainstream media as if they were
actual news items being reported on by journalists. Some items appear as
local news; often public relations professionals act as if they were reporters.
With critics actively excluded from the packaging, key issues such as
Iraq and Medicare reform can be misrepresented, creating a false perception
amongst the audience that they are viewing genuine, factual news.[14] In
essence, Americans are routinely subjected not just to ideologically
restricted viewpoints, but to actual pre-packaged propaganda despite
explicit laws forbidding domestic propaganda.

Despite the revelations on this practice by the *New York Times*,
the US government seems undeterred. Under intense criticism, the Pentagon
was forced to close its Office of Strategic Influence,[15] intended to plant fake
stories in foreign media—including in allied nations—to present a more
pro-American message, without disclosing the US government as the
source, but it continues to return to the project[16] As relations between the
US and Iran deteriorate further, stories that fit the line of the Bush
Administration's position are appearing more regularly without scrutiny.[17]

Such practices are not new. As J.W. Smith notes, fake news was
integral to the Cold War since the 50s and 60s.[18] Not only were think
tanks, universities, and other institutions often unwittingly disseminating
planted stories and ideas, but there is a high likelihood that they have
been passing on similar propaganda produced by earlier similarly motivated
agents, resulting in the building throughout history of "frameworks of
orientation" and "social control belief systems" to gain or maintain
support of the masses.

Propaganda

Propaganda is easier to identify in other countries, especially those
with totalitarian regimes, because the direct influence of the government

on the news-making process is recognized. However, the sources of a similar achievement of journalistic conformity in one's own country seem harder to recognize. Australian journalist John Pilger captured the essence of this some time ago:

> Long before the Soviet Union broke up, a group of Russian writers touring the United States were astonished to find, after reading the newspapers and watching television, that almost all the opinions on all the vital issues were the same. "In our country," said one of them, "to get that result we have a dictatorship. We imprison people. We tear out their fingernails. Here you have none of that. How do you do it? What's the secret?"[19]

In recent decades, before the War on Terror, propaganda was a regular feature of media content. For example, the Center for Defense Information (CDI), an organization consisting of many ex-senior military personnel, noted that arms manufacturers often employed fear of others to create and justify increased arms spending. Their tactics almost mirrored those of the "peddlers of crisis" that had been sharply criticized by the League of Nations decades earlier. A documentary from the CDI noted in 1997 that the arms industry was actively pushing for newer weaponry and military technologies, portraying the F-22 as an anti-war plane, justifying military spending because it would create jobs (even if in reality some of the jobs would be abroad with countries who purchased the arms and planes), and creating a sense of awe with breathtaking air shows.[20] Popular films have also been subject to "altered history and amended scripts at the request of the Pentagon," including Top Gun, Armageddon and Pearl Harbor.[21]

Media, Propaganda, and Vietnam

In Vietnam, the manufactured/exaggerated "Gulf of Tonkin" incident was used as a pretext for the US to go to war. In fact, the "Gulf of Tonkin Resolution" was drawn up by the US two months before the attack.[22]

Public support for the war only faded when belated stories of massacres by US forces came to light, typically portrayed as "mistakes" or "blunders." The My Lai massacre was headlined as "AN AMERICAN TRAGEDY" in *Newsweek*, not a Vietnamese tragedy. Despite the common belief that the mainstream media lost the war for the US, in actuality it generally supported it but just debated the tactics.[23]

As J.W. Smith noted, "It is said that America lost in Vietnam but 3 million people were slaughtered ..., millions of acres of forest poisoned with herbicides were destroyed and, after winning its freedom, Vietnam was further decimated by embargoes."[24]

And after all that, "Vietnam has been compensating the United States. In 1997 it began to pay off about $145 million in debts left by the defeated South Vietnamese government for American food and infrastructure aid. Thus, Hanoi is reimbursing the United States for part of the cost of the war waged against it."[25]

Media, Propaganda, and Iraq

Propaganda helped justify the first US-Iraq Gulf War in 1991. Scare stories were created that portrayed Saddam Hussein's invasion of Kuwait as the precursor of a regional or global ambition, and so it was easy to invoke images of the need to fight a new Hitler. As *The Christian Science Monitor* later reported, the main justification for the war—the Iraqi troop build-up along the Kuwait and Saudi Arabia border—was a lie. When satellite image and desert military experts reviewed the "smoking gun" images, they saw a build-up of US military fighter jets, not an Iraqi troop build up.[26]

When the first Iraq war offered dramatic footage of "smart" precision bombs, awe at our technical capacity was inevitable amongst the American audience. Yet we rarely had visited upon us the shock that some 70,000 Iraqis may have died from war-related damages to infrastructure in the wake of our assault.[27] Instead, we were treated to the infamous story of Iraqi soldiers killing babies in Kuwait by switching off baby incubators, given heightened credibility by a young Kuwaiti nurse crying in front of the cameras. In reality, the 15 year-old girl was the daughter of the Kuwaiti ambassador to Washington. She had not been to Kuwait in years, and was part of a public relations stunt set up by the Hill and Knowlton firm to help create support for a war by fostering disgust and animosity towards Iraq.

The subsequent sanctions enforced by the US and UK were estimated to have killed some 200,000-500,000 children (possibly a similar number of adults). The constant bombing sorties by US/UK forces were rarely reported. Most of us were unaware of the immense hardship on the Iraqi people, and the thorough containment of Saddam Hussein. This made it easier to put most of the blame for the negative effects of sanctions onto Saddam—and indeed on the Iraqi victims themselves, who in the view of many American mainstream political commentators should have overthrown him but failed to do so.[28]

The biggest lie, perhaps, was that Iraq had weapons of mass destruction ready for deployment. Before 2003 officials repeatedly reminded us that Saddam Hussein had used WMDs against his own people in the past. Rarely were such officials challenged as to why we had not done something at that time, when he was an ally of the West (against the common foe, Iran) and when Western countries had provided such capabilities in the first place.

A study by Johns Hopkins University, published in the *Lancet*, found that the Bush/Blair-led 2003 Iraq invasion may have caused 400,000 to 950,000 deaths since the war was declared by Bush as having *ended*. The numbers were so shocking that President Bush simply rejected them as lacking credibility and using discredited practices, even though the peer-reviewed study used established practices for measuring mortality in poor countries (a technique used by the US government, the UN and others). The media never challenged Bush when he rejected the findings or on the relative merits of the studies when Bush referred instead to a casualty value that was similar to the Iraq Body Count's estimate (30,000 to 60,000 deaths), a non peer-reviewed account based on casualties actually reported by the Western mainstream press.[29]

The decade-long global propaganda and public relations campaign by the Rendon Group, a self-styled "international strategic communications consultancy providing real-time solutions to public and private sector clients worldwide", was eventually revealed by *The New Yorker*. Fake stories had been planted in the domestic and international press. "It was amazing how well it worked. It was like magic," exclaimed the Rendon Group publicist. Linking Saddam Hussein to terrorist organizations as a public manipulation strategy succeeded because "the war was largely marketed domestically as a scare campaign." The fear of September 11 was easy to exploit.[30]

Conclusion

The departure from reality in recent years, at the hands of government or media or both, has become a great concern. The aforementioned public relations stunt in 1990 of the young Kuwaiti girl accusing Iraqi soldiers of killing babies in a hospital angered enough people to support a disastrous war. In 2002 the Downing Street Memo summarized a meeting between George Bush and Tony Blair in which it became clear that "Bush had made up his mind to take military action, even if the timing was not yet decided."[31] In 2003 Jessica Lynch became a hero for an escape from Iraqi soldiers until it was learned that her adventure was filmed by the Defense Department with guns and blanks and props, like the Hollywood movie 'Black Hawk Down.' It was "one of the most stunning pieces of news management ever conceived," the *BBC* reported.[32] In 2005 the U.S. State Department, with terrorism on the rise, stopped publishing its annual report on terrorism.[33] What's next? Here might be a clue: In 2007, a Congressional Research Service report stated that the United States "may face no greater challenge from a single country than Iran."[34]

The constant claim that the US has the freest press in the world is accepted almost without question, even as *Reporters without Borders* ranks US press freedom quite low compared to many other countries in the world: ranking just 48th in their 2007 Press Freedom Index.[35]

Such perceptions are possible when a concentrated media represents the public less than the interests of those in power—and indeed when part of its propaganda mission is to assure you that it's free.

Further Reading

Bagdikian, Ben, *The Media Monopoly*, Boston: Beacon Press, Sixth Edition, 2000.

Chomsky, Noam and Herman, Edward, *Manufacturing Consent*, New York: Pantheon Press, 1986, 2002.

Knightley, Phillip, *The First Casualty: The War Correspondent as Hero, Propagandist and Myth-Maker*, London: Andre Deutsch Ltd., 1975, revised 2003.

McChesney, Robert W, *Rich Media, Poor Democracy; Communication Politics in Dubious Times*, University of Illinois Press, 1999.

Smith, J.W, *Economic Democracy: The Political Struggle for the 21st Century, 4th Edition*, Cambria: Institute for Economic Democracy Press, 2005.

Web sites for further information

* http://www.globalissues.org The web site from this chapter's author which covers many of the above issues in further depth.

* http://www.fair.org Fairness and Accuracy In Reporting (FAIR), provides timely analysis and alerts into various issues surrounding US mainstream media.

* http://www.democracynow.org A radio and TV broadcast looking at issues that the mainstream often fails to cover.

* http://www.medialens.org A British media watch dog providing detailed analysis of mainstream media short-comings.

- http://www.stopbigmedia.com The StopBigMedia.com coalition is campaigning to stop the FCC from allowing a handful of giant corporations to dominate the America's media system.
- http://www.ied.info The Institute for Economic Democracy provides detailed historical context, including how propaganda and "social control belief systems" fits into that.
- http://www.prwatch.org PR Watch, from the Center for Media and Democracy attempts to monitor and highlight public relations spin and propaganda.
- http://www.cjr.org Columbia Journalism Review looks at various aspects of journalism., Illinois: University of Illinois Press, 1999.

Despite serious questions as to his past military service, President Bush presented himself in full flight gear when, aboard the aircraft carrier USS Abraham Lincoln, he declared combat operations over in Iraq. Bush later claimed that the Mission Accomplished sign which memorialized this speech had been put up by members of the Lincoln's Crew. The next day, the White House admitted that it had helped with the production of a 'Mission Accomplished' banner as a backdrop.

September 11, 2001. George Bush after being informed of the second strike on the World Trade Towers while reading from *My Pet Goat* to Florida schoolchildren.

SELF-AWARENESS

We Understand How War Affects Us

Do we understand the meaning and impact of war?

In Vietnam we believed we were driven by the moral objective of defeating the evil presence of Communism. Yet the 15-year struggle ended with no clear winner. In the 1990 Gulf War we marveled at the power and precision of our superior air forces, and we took pride in our singular goal of liberating the besieged country of Kuwait. The current Iraq War has once again left our nation questioning its role in an increasingly interdependent world. War correspondent Chris Hedges describes the 'Myth of War' — the belief, as in Vietnam, that we were fighting for the moral objective of defeating the evil presence of Communism. We build up a hatred for the other side that blinds us to the similarities between warring nations. In *War Is a Force That Gives Us Meaning*, Hedges states: "In mythic war we imbue events with meanings they do not have. We see defeats as signposts on the road to ultimate victory. We demonize the enemy so that our opponent is no longer human. We view ourselves, our people, as the embodiment of absolute goodness."[1]

A 2003 study by Harvard University's Dominic Johnson proposes that the phenomenon of 'positive illusions' may contribute to an exaggerated belief, especially among men, that they will be successful in situations such as war.[2] This may explain the willingness of greatly outnumbered forces to go to battle, and often to achieve victory. In the 16th century the Spanish explorer Pizarro and 168 men used superior weapons and the element of surprise to defeat 80,000 Incan soldiers. General Erwin Rommel was known for winning battles against apparently much stronger opponents. On the other hand, the Korean War dragged on because of General MacArthur's underestimation of the Chinese, and the British had similarly disregarded the skills and intensity of Japanese soldiers in World War 2.

The positive illusion allows us to justify actions that are damnable if done by others. For example, in the 1950s the U.S. installed a missile base in Turkey that was within range of the Soviet Union. Soon after, when the Soviet Union attempted to install a similar base in Cuba, we threatened war to prevent such a hostile and unjustifiable affront. In 1970 the U.S. bombed Cambodia because it provided supply routes to communist North Vietnam, but we condemned Nicaragua's invasion of Honduras when the contra rebels used that neighboring country for its supply routes. And today, we seek to deny Iran's right under the Nuclear Non-Proliferation Treaty to pursue nuclear energy development, while we stockpile nuclear weapons and tolerate the same from our allies in Israel and India.

The positive illusion may have emboldened our current administration in its war on Iraq, even in the face of powerful evidence against the prospects for success. As noted earlier in the book, studies by our own government have confirmed that the occupation of Iraq has increased the terrorism threat. Our military has underestimated the resolve of nationalistic Iraqi insurgents, and as a result our *mission accomplished* of May 1, 2003 may have become an unachievable mission.

The positive illusion is magnified by our distance from the war. We remain in our comfortable homes, safe from any real danger, content to read about the war as we do the sports section. We feel we have the best team and that we'll win in the end. But we don't see the war as our young soldiers do. We don't see the slaughter of human beings on their own soil for reasons that grow less clear over time. We don't sense the desperation of patriots who have little else to live for than to repel foreign invaders who desecrate their homeland. We don't see the folly of fighting insurgents with massive firepower, as if we were attacking a swarm of insects with our fists. Many of us aren't aware of these details of war, for we have jobs and families and the future to think about. We don't have time for war.

6

ILLUSION
War doesn't impact me personally.

REALITY
**War impacts me economically, culturally, socially,
politically and spiritually.**

Maureen Dolan

> A human being is part of a whole, called by us the
> "Universe," a part limited in time and space. (S)he
> experiences self, thoughts and feelings, as something
> separated from the rest—a kind of optical delusion of
> consciousness. This delusion is a kind of prison for
> us, restricting us to our personal desires and to
> affection for a few persons nearest us. Our task must
> be to free ourselves from this prison by widening our
> circles of compassion to embrace all living creatures
> and the whole of nature in its beauty.
> **—Albert Einstein**

Americans' lives are consumed with caring for families, jobs,
schoolwork, careers, and recreation. Our time is taken up with a plethora
of minutiae: filling the car with gas, getting the kids to school, paying our
bills, fixing up our homes, dealing with health issues, answering emails,
faxes, phones, etc. We live in a speeded-up world where multi-tasking has
eroded our powers of concentration and leaves us suffering from the
effects of stress. Our thoughts come and go at lightning speed. While
many thoughts we have about ourselves or others or the world are based
in reality, other thoughts are culturally conditioned beliefs we hold to—
even when evidence proves the contrary.

One of the illusions that many Americans have held in the past is
now in the process of dissolving: that *war doesn't impact me personally.*
People cling to this illusion out of fear and ignorance, seeking to avoid
even the suffering caused simply by thinking about war—as if what we
don't know won't hurt us. We find excuses in feelings of powerlessness;
we willfully overlook not just the possibility but the proven fact that

elected officials could lie to us. We feel we can just slip on by, neglect our responsibilities as citizens in a democracy, and disregard the connections between our individual existence and the wider social reality. We delude ourselves with the notion that this forgetfulness of our true nature as human and spiritual beings is without cost—to ourselves or to others.

As our awareness increases, however, we realize that *war does impact me personally.* A new and profound companion thought also dawns upon us: *Peace impacts me personally.*

What is the cause of our increased awareness—simply that our altruism and thoughtfulness has increased? Or is it that we start to see the signs of deepening malaise everywhere around us?

The Economic Impact

For many of us, our financial situations already cause us a great deal of stress. Earning a living in the U.S. has become more complicated in the 21st century and we push away thoughts of how war affects us because we have more immediate problems—we think—on our minds. However, our financial situation is intimately connected to how the U.S. allocates its resources.

If you look at your taxes, you will see Americans are contributing more and more money to financing wars. On average, each American has already paid more than $4,000.[1] The Iraq war alone has now cost the American taxpayers as a whole nearly $500 billion—and still counting. According to the Nobel Prize-winning economist and Colombia University Professor, Joseph Stiglitz, the estimated total cost of our present wars will exceed 2.2 trillion dollars.[2] Part of this is from the taxes we pay now and part of it is mounting up into an enormous debt we are putting on the next generation.

The wealth of our nation has been taken out of our pockets, out of our schools, out of job creation, affordable housing, healthcare, alternative energy sources, public transit, the decaying infrastructure of our cities, roads and bridges, etc. and transferred into the pockets of oil companies, military contractors, and armament manufacturers. Whether you are seeking a good education for yourself or your children, or are concerned about whether your income can or will be able to meet your future needs, or even simply if you care about the cost of food and gas—then war impacts you personally. What your government is spending on wars could have been spent on projects for the public good, or left in your own pockets to address your own pressing needs.

The National Priorities Project[3] provides a breakdown by state and congressional district on the human and financial costs of the Iraq War.[4] It also shows what a half trillion in Iraq War spending could buy each congressional district in local services. Citing from this rich resource, let's take a look at Democratic Majority Leader Nancy Pelosi's Congressional district in California. The war cost her district $1.18 billion. For that money, health care could have been provided to 109,712 children for the length of the Iraq war; 3,522 housing units could have been built, or 89 elementary schools. If you want to see what it cost your local district, just check this resource out.

Since the beginning of the wars against Afghanistan and Iraq, millions of Americans have lost their health insurance. We live in the only industrialized country in the world where 1 out of 6 does not have healthcare coverage (nearly 50 million Americans). As the US pursues wars of "preemptive strikes" to control oil resources, the introduction of extreme violence into areas that possess oil means that oil prices shoot up. Iraqi oil production has yet to return to pre-war levels. We not only feel that at the gas pump but also in higher food costs and raised costs for all consumer goods.

Photographer: shooterguy Copyright: Lawrence Sawyer

Bridge No. 9340, Minnesota's busiest, had been classified as "structurally deficient" by state bridge inspectors as have 77,000 aging bridges nationwide. (*Washington Post*, August 3, 2007). Thirty-four percent of America's major roads are in poor or mediocre condition. Twenty-seven percent of America's bridges are structurally deficient or functionally obsolete.

The Cultural Impact

The dominant culture in the U.S glorifies individualism, accumulation of wealth, and violence as a way to solve problems and fulfill needs. Even though the wars for oil are taking place thousands of miles away, the mistaken idea that violence is a solution to problems—or that if we need something, we can just take it, whether it belongs to us or not—impacts each one of us in our homes, our schools, our communities. There is hardly an American alive now that has not known someone who has been the victim of violence. This is the kind of indicator one typically uses to measure the extent of casualties in military conflicts.

As government violence in the form of war is accepted, domestic violence increases. Militarism in our culture promotes violence in families and at the community level. The leading cause of death of pregnant women in the US is murder by a boyfriend or spouse. Twenty-five percent of women have experienced violence in the home. In 2006, there were 30,000 gunshot victims in a country with 200 million guns. In fact, the biggest terror attack in America before 9/11 was carried out by an American (Timothy McVeigh) who trained in the military and fought in the Gulf War.

Militarism requires a simplification of situations, a restriction of the range of options, a division into operational "sides" and a blindness to consequences. As we have leaders, media, and even intellectuals who explicitly talk in terms of "the good guys" and "the bad guys", we lose our grip on the nuances of human motivation, to say nothing of their social causes. Our movies come to resemble or are drawn from our cartoons, we seek out super-heroes, and on the darker lower end, in chop 'em up movies, a raw blood-lust is unleashed. Our television is debased by endless "cop-shows", where vicariously we watch as the righteous police hunt down their irredeemable prey.

War is an invention, as the cultural anthropologist Margaret Mead pointed out.[5] It was NOT always with us and can be abolished. In those cultures and countries that have rejected war, the violence in their own societies is diminished. When a culture embraces diplomacy, conflict resolution, and the cultivation of non-violent means to solve problems, then the incidents of home-grown violence go down. One way to do this would be to establish a U.S. Department of Peace, as proposed in Congress by Rep. Dennis Kucinich, which would put the cultural emphasis on training in non-violent tactics as a way to solve problems in both the domestic and international spheres (see the Peace Alliance).[6] Peace towards other countries is directly connected to the peace within our own country and impacts each of us personally. For our own safety and sanity, it is time for a paradigm shift.

The Social Impact

The majority of Americans have never experienced war directly. We don't know what it feels like to have bombs dropping on us, to have our arms or legs blown off, to have our best buddies next to us lose their lives. Yet, over the next few years, many of us will meet at least one of the one million service people who have served in Afghanistan or Iraq. They are our co-workers, neighbors, friends, and relatives. It is estimated that at least one third of the returning military personnel will experience Post Traumatic Stress Disorder (PTSD) or Traumatic Brain Injuries (TBI). Missing limbs are also prevalent among returning vets, numbering in the tens of thousands. The rate of homelessness among Vietnam vets reached gigantic proportions after that war ended and their suicide rate was much higher than the number of those killed in combat in that war. Already there are at least 1,000 homeless Iraq vets in our society and the suicide rate for returning vets is climbing. For more information on veterans, see Iraq Veterans Against the War,[7] Appeal for Redress,[8] and Thank You Lt. Ehren Watada[9].

The 2007 scandal surrounding Walter Reed Hospital in DC, which exposed the mistreatment of our injured veterans, is only the tip of the iceberg. In spite of much rhetoric about "supporting our troops," the people who promote war do not similarly promote caring for the wounded troops arriving home. In fact, when it comes to caring for our troops, the most diligent and most robust voices for benefits for our veterans are veterans and peace groups—the very people who are condemned for not supporting them. They are testifying in Congress, forming support groups, trying to find psychological and financial help for those impacted directly by war.

Beyond the social realities that war will bring home to America, there is the social reality of those in the countries we have attacked. Presently, two million Iraqis have had to flee their own country to escape war. Another two million are displaced within Iraq. All the terror and hardships that face the Iraqi people are carried with them into uncertain futures and have wide implications for the entire world.

The Political Impact

There has never been a war that did not impact the political realities of the society that waged that war. War always exacerbates the divisions in a society because rights are restricted in wartime and resources are diverted to the war effort. In the last few years, we have witnessed a huge restructuring of America's democratic institutions. It has led to an imbalance of power and a constitutional crisis. This has important effects on every American.

The attacks on our democracy have come in the form of abuses of the "Patriot Act," the undermining of habeas corpus, government expansion of spying on Americans, growth of mercenary armies like Blackwater, the use of extraordinary rendition, the promotion of torture, and the violation of the Geneva Conventions and other international treaties. It is not only the Democrats and Republicans elected to office who bear responsibility for this. The guarantees under the US Constitution depend upon the awareness of, and participation of, its populace to breathe life into the freedoms we espouse. History has shown that it is possible for a democracy to lose its way if power is concentrated in the hands of the few. There have been democratic republics that were usurped by dictators after human rights were steadily eroded.

In spite of the huge propaganda efforts by the US government and the corporate owned media to rush to war, there were voices from independent media and peace groups that spoke the truth to power. In just the last few years, because of the creative and sustained efforts of those exercising their democratic rights, we have witnessed a striking increase in the percentage of Americans who want to halt war.[10] According to a *New York Times* poll of May 2007, 72% of Americans say that the country is on the wrong track and 61% say that the US should have stayed out of Iraq. This is an enormous change.

Even if you once thought that war didn't impact you personally, you can still impact the ability of your country to wage war against others and restrict rights at home, just as those speaking out against the war have now proved. If we are not protesting our government's policy of war by writing letters to our Senators and Congresspeople or letters to the editors of newspapers or marching for peace or working with others in groups to educate and organize about war and peace, or even just donating money so that others can do so, then we are giving our quiet approval. We are complicit.

No democratic nation can go to war without the consent of the governed. We, as citizens, have the power to elect representatives to do our bidding. We have the power to replace those representatives we have elected with others, if they break their commitments to us once elected. Without our agreement to send our tax money for war, without our permission to send our sons and daughters to war, no war can be fought. It's an extraordinary power of democracy we wield, if only we recognize it.

The Environmental Impact

War impacts each one of us by its contribution to climate change. The vast amount of oil burned to fuel warplanes, war ships, armored vehicles, etc. sends tons more of carbon dioxide into the atmosphere. Even though the US is only about 4% of the world population, we use more than 25% of the world's fossil fuels. Scientists are now united on the human impact of global warming (For more information, see the Intergovernmental Panel on Climate Change.)[11] The 70 million tons of carbon dioxide we release into our atmosphere every 24 hours is already having dire consequences due to the "greenhouse effect." There are already millions of people experiencing severe droughts and floods;

millions more climate change refugees are expected in future years as food sources and clean water dry up. The oceans are rising but the fresh water sources are being depleted. Species are disappearing at an alarming rate; the intensity of storms has increased; diseases are spreading. It's a grievous irony that the US is responsible for people dying in wars in order to secure oil fields and pipelines just when we have come to the realization that the use of petroleum is killing our planet.

War also hurts the environment by polluting or destroying fresh water sources. War hurts the environment by the use of depleted uranium. War hurts the environment by the unexploded ordnance left behind that continues to explode long after the war has ended. In addition to this, the *Bulletin of Atomic Scientists* determined that the world is even closer to the danger of nuclear war and recently moved its "doomsday clock" to register five minutes to midnight.[12]

The International Ramifications

The introduction of violence into the Mideast by US wars of invasion and occupation have succeeded in increasing terror attacks by astronomical proportions. There is no way to wage war against a tactic. War itself is terror. It is not our freedom or "way of life" that inspires the tactic of terrorism. Rather, our polices of domination and violence have made the world distrust Americans and fostered an increase of terrorism.[13]

Americans will be safer at home and abroad when we understand the causes of current wars and work to change the foreign policy of the United States.[14] Our personal security is tied up with the international situation. So, it is up to us to expand our awareness of the world situation by discussion with others and reading a broad array of foreign and domestic media. Websites like truthout.org, commondreams.org, and informationclearinghouse.info are especially helpful.

The Spiritual Impact

War has changed drastically over the last century. One hundred years ago soldiers met on the battlefields and fought each other. War was considered inevitable by the world's people then but all this has changed with the growth of consciousness and the development of technology. While civilian casualties occurred in WWI, they dramatically increased in WWII. In the 1980s, civilian casualties of wars (such as the US wars in Central America) took a huge jump to 80%. And now, over 90% of those killed in wars are civilians, with the majority being women and children. The US war against Vietnam proved that there can be no invasion and occupation without genocide (three million South Asians killed in a decade). A study by Johns Hopkins University and published in the British Medical

Journal *Lancet*, now estimates that 655,000 people have died in the war on Iraq.[15] For all of us who contribute to the funding and/or tacit approval of war, this is a heavy and tragic karmic burden.

With the victories of non-violence that the world witnessed in the 20th century—the independence of India, the abolition of apartheid in South Africa, the overthrow of Marcos in the Philippines, the defeat of fascism in Argentina and Chile, the victory of Solidarity in Poland (whose leadership then ushered in neoliberalism and who are now hated), the breakup of the Soviet Union, etc.—the people of the world can now see that war is obsolete.[16] Big changes can occur with peaceful means. As Gandhi said, "We are constantly being astonished these days at the amazing discoveries in the field of violence. But I maintain that far more undreamt of and seemingly impossible discoveries will be made in the field of nonviolence."[17]

War does not impact us only in the economic, cultural, social, political, environmental and international spheres; our spiritual realities are at stake. No matter what your particular faith tradition is, it cannot justify the immense slaughter of women and children or the destruction of our planet.

The spiritual heritage of humanity is clear: The Prophet Muhammad said: "That person is the most beloved of God who does most good to God's creatures."[18] From the Judeo-Christian commandment of "Thou shall not kill" to the Christian precept of loving one's neighbor and the enunciation by Jesus of the Beatitudes to the Hindu directive of Ahimsa (non-violence), the core of all faith traditions teaches peace. The Buddha said: "The thought manifests as the word; the word manifests as the deed; the deed develops into habit; and habit hardens into character. So watch the thought and its ways with care; and let it spring from love born out of concern for all beings."[19]

In conclusion, we must face this: To ignore facts of our own reality is to invite ignorance and suffering into our lives. We are facing global crises of climate change, the growing gap between the haves and the have-nots, the struggle for clean water and energy. Either we will be contributing to war or we will be contributing to peace. The invasions and occupations of Afghanistan and Iraq by our country at the start of the 21st century and the peaceful resistance to these wars by millions of the world's people were only the beginning. As Americans, we live in the largest military power on earth and bear a special responsibility to end wars being waged against people and the planet itself.

To think that "war or peace doesn't impact on me" is to be in a state of denial about the complex effects of interconnectedness and responsibility—the connections within individuals to our own bodies, minds, and spirits, of individuals within their societies, and in turn of their societies within the global community.

Further Reading

Barash, David, ed. *Approaches to Peace*. New York: Oxford UP, 2000.

Gandhi, M.K. Dear, John, ed. *Mohandas Gandhi: Essential Writings*. New York: Orbis, 2005.

Huther, Gerald. *The Compassionate Brain: How Empathy Creates Intelligence*. Boston: Trumpeter, 2006.

Klare, Michael T. *Blood and Oil: The Dangers and Consequences of America's Growing Dependency on Imported Petroleum*. New York: Henry Holt, 2004.

Korten, David C. *The Great Turning: From Empire to Earth Community*. San Francisco: Berret-Koehler and Bloomfield CT: Kumarian Press, 2006.

Pape, Robert A.. *Dying to Win: The Strategic Logic of Suicide Terrorism*. New York: Random House, 2005.

Roberts, Elizabeth and Amidon, Elias. *Life Prayers From Around the World*. San Francisco: Harper, 1996.

Sharp, Gene. *Waging Nonviolent Struggle: 20th Century Practice And 21st Century Potential*. Boston: Porter Sargent Publishers Inc.,

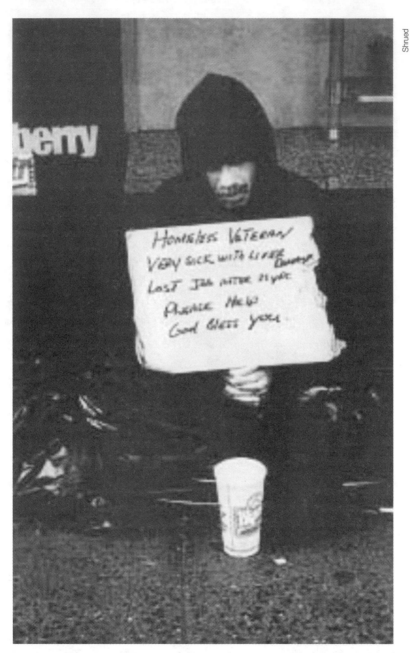

Current population estimates suggest that about 195,000 veterans (male and female) are homeless on any given night. Source: United States Department of Veterans Affairs, http://www1.va.gov/homeless/page.cfm?pg=1

7

ILLUSION

The military will take good care of our soldiers.

REALITY

Our soldiers return home with physical and mental injuries that are largely ignored.

Tod Ensign

"Support for our veterans has been a high priority. My current proposed budget will increase VA health care spending 83% since I took office. The Pentagon's health care budget has grown from $19 to $38 billion."

George W. Bush
American Legion National Convention
March 6, 2007

Bush's speech follows the time-honored custom whereby American Presidents make grandiose but vague promises about their dedication to the needs of military veterans. His boast that he has increased health care spending for both the VA and the armed services doesn't mean much. After all, the military has wasted billions of dollars in Iraq with little or nothing to show for it. It currently takes the VA more than a year to process a routine disability claim. Over half of the Army's 36 medical centers were recently criticized for failing to comply with an Army requirement that routine medical care be provided within seven days.[1]

America's military veterans have always had to fight for adequate medical care and disability compensation for their service-connected injuries from a recalcitrant federal government. It took fifteen years of political agitation by Vietnam vets before Congress finally ordered the VA to establish a disability system that would automatically compensate them for certain medical problems and cancers caused by their exposure to "Agent Orange", the toxic herbicide that the US military dumped all over southern Vietnam.

Veterans who were exposed to low-level ionizing radiation during A bomb tests conducted both at the Nevada test site and in the South

Pacific during the 1940s and 50s have had even less success in getting the VA to compensate them for their radiation-induced cancers and other health problems.

In April, 2007 the Pentagon reported that the suicide rate for military personnel in 2006 was 17.3 per 100,000 compared to a rate of 11 per 100,000 among civilians. The rate for 2005 was even higher—19.4 per hundred thousand. A VA associate director reported that 5,000 veterans now commit suicide each year, including 1,000 failed suicides who are currently under the VA's care.[2]

Trained to Kill: The Culture of Trauma

The soldier's real work is killing.
—Dr. Theodore Nadelson[3]

Fighting wars has always caused mental illness among some soldiers. During the Civil War, this mental condition was dubbed, "soldier's heart." During the First World War, the term "shell shock" came into use only to be replaced by "battle fatigue" during the Second World War. It wasn't until 1980 that the American Psychiatric Association adopted "post traumatic stress disorder" (PTSD) as a formal medical diagnosis. Since then, both the military and VA have accepted, at least in theory, that PTSD is a medical condition which merits both treatment and, where appropriate, disability compensation.

Because of the nature of the fighting most American troops experience in Iraq and Afghanistan, some therapists believe that they will eventually develop far higher rates of PTSD and other mental disorders than soldiers in earlier wars. There are two reasons for this. First, GIs today serve much longer periods in combat zones than did soldiers in Vietnam, where one twelve-month tour was standard. Many soldiers today are serving their second or even third combat tour—plus each tour was recently lengthened from 12 to 15 months.

Second, waging counter-insurgency warfare can bring on greater combat stress because it's more difficult for soldiers to distinguish between combatants and non-combatants. This kind of fighting results in GIs inadvertently injuring or killing many innocent civilians, including women and children.

More than a third of combat troops returning from Iraq and Afghanistan have been diagnosed with a mental or "psychosocial" disorder, according to a recent study, "Bringing the War Back Home." published in the Archives of Internal Medicine by researchers from the University of California-San Francisco. Out of the 103,788 vets assessed by VA examiners, 32,000 were found to have mental health problems, with

13,200 receiving a diagnosis of PTSD. The report concludes that "veterans aged 18-24 were at the greatest risk for suffering from mental illness" and that "early detection and intervention...were needed to prevent chronic mental illness and disability."[4]

Veterans' Medical Needs Overwhelm the System

Advances in the military's ability to treat combat injuries means that today many soldiers survive wounds that would have been fatal in earlier wars. Thus, thousands of severely disabled vets, many with traumatic brain injuries, are returning home and will require intensive medical care — often for the rest of their lives.

The Response: Arranging Deck Chairs on the Titanic

Deaf to a growing drumbeat of criticism, James Nicholson, then Secretary of Veterans Affairs, remained clueless during a May 2007 hearing of the House Veterans Committee; "The VA is adequately staffed to take care of the mission that we have. I think that the VA healthcare system is doing an extraordinary job," he testified. Committee Chair U.S. Rep. Bob Filner (D-CA) responded with incredulity; "If you said that in any veterans' town meeting that any of us have led, they would have laughed you off the stage!"[5]

Nicholson offered no explanation for an internal VA survey which found that vet walk-ins from the Iraq and Afghan wars at its storefront "Vet Centers" had more than doubled, from 8,965 in 2004 to 21,681 in 2006, while clinic staff had increased by less than 10%. The survey also found that while 114 of the 209 centers reported a need for at least one extra psychologist or therapist to deal with the influx, the VA planned to add only 61 new staff.[6]

"Suck It Up and Drive On!" Seeking Psychiatric Help Is Risky for GIs

Every first sergeant in Iraq uses this phrase to mock or belittle soldiers whom he or she believes is griping or complaining without good cause. Unfortunately, when this sort of macho peer pressure is directed at soldiers who are suffering from post traumatic stress disorder it can have serious, even fatal, consequences.

There have been numerous stories in the media about Iraq and Afghanistan vets who chose, with tragic results, to ignore intense feelings of depression because they feared that seeking mental health care would end their careers.

Just outside the gates of Ft Drum, NY a military family has erected a home-made memorial/shrine arranged around a tree that was hit by an NCO in November, 2006 a few weeks after he returned from Iraq. One emotional touch is a cross erected by his children which spells out "Dad" in blue and white flowers. The First Sergeant, who had spent the night drinking before hitting the tree at an estimated 120 mph, was killed instantly.

The first signs of serious stress are often nightmares or an inability to sleep. Other symptoms include suicidal ideation, loss of pleasure in once-joyous activities like playing with one's children, hyper-arousal, increased anger, emotional outbursts, and reliance on alcohol and/or drugs to "self medicate."

If a soldier acknowledges that he or she needs help dealing with emotional problems, what impact will this have on their military career in the future? If a GI who was trained to fight with an infantry, armor or artillery unit is given a "medical profile" for PTSD from a medical board, he or she will likely face involuntary discharge action, or at least a bar to re-enlistment. After all, if a disability prevents a combat soldier from being able to "do the job," what value does he or she continue to have to the military?

"Going on the Economy": Seeking Care in the Civilian Sector

Roughly one third of returning soldiers seek out mental health counseling during their first year home. Frustrated by long waiting lists for psychological treatment on military bases, many GIs and their dependents have been seeking treatment from private therapists and clinics—only to encounter new obstacles.

Many private mental clinics and therapists refuse to accept the military Tri Care medical insurance, citing its low reimbursement rates and tangle of red tape. The Tri care office serving Ft Campbell and Ft. Bragg—military posts with heavy deployment rates, told an Army study group that it routinely heard from soldiers complaining about the difficulty of finding therapists who accept Tri Care. Over 9.1 million soldiers and dependents are currently covered by the program—up one million since 2001.[7]

Seeking Recognition of Disability

Both the military and the VA have their own bureaucratic systems for processing disability claims of soldiers and veterans. Although separate, the systems are closely linked, especially where documentation of disability claims is concerned.

Often when solders are preparing to leave the military they don't understand the importance of documenting their injury or exposure while still on active duty. For example, some GIs who claimed they were harmed by the military's controversial anthrax vaccine program later discovered that the inoculations hadn't been accurately recorded in their medical records.[8]

Tens of thousands of World War Two and Korean War vets discovered years after the fact that no one had entered information in their military records about radiation exposure levels they'd received while participating as "observers" to over fifty nuclear bomb tests, both in the South Pacific and at the Nevada test site.

Years after the war ended, Vietnam vets learned that many of them had been exposed in Vietnam to Agent Orange, a herbicide which contained minuscule amounts of TCDD-dioxin, the most toxic synthetic compound known. Their efforts to win compensation for cancers and other ailments attributed to this exposure were unsuccessful because they had no records of exposure. After years of debate, Congress finally made it possible for some vets to win disability by requiring a presumption of exposure and ordering the VA to create disease-categories which would be presumed "service connected."[9]

Post Traumatic Stress in an Iraq War Vet: A Case Study

Several mental health professionals have predicted that the number of soldiers returning from Iraq and Afghanistan who will develop PTSD and other mental disorders will climb to unprecedented levels in the years ahead.

One Iraq vet, Sp/4 Eugene Cherry was recently discharged, ending a two year battle with his command at Ft Drum, NY to obtain effective psychological treatment for his PTSD condition. Eugene had served thirteen months as a combat medic in Iraq, dealing with horrific injuries and deaths to soldiers and Iraqi civilians on a daily basis. When he began to experience sleep disturbance and flashbacks, he sought psychological care in Iraq. Except for a few brief consultations with military psychologists, the military's preferred mode of treatment was to give him Effexor, Paxel and Zoloft, all powerful anti depressants. None of these relieved his symptoms, leaving him still sleepless and painfully anxious.[10]

Eugene hoped that once he returned with his unit to Ft Drum, in upstate New York, he would begin to receive psychological treatment for his PTSD which continued unabated. But, once again he was given anti-depressant drugs—instead of psychotherapy.

A few weeks after returning to Drum, Eugene went home to Chicago on leave. While staying at his mother's he found that he rarely slept more than a couple of hours a night and that his temper was on hair trigger. He fixated on memories of mutilated victims of car bombings in Iraq whom he'd treated as a medic. He was eventually referred to Dr.

Hannah Frisch, a civilian psychologist, who treated him without fee and eventually provided him with a formal diagnosis: post traumatic stress disorder. In early 2007, Eugene finally returned to Ft Drum, expecting that he would be given a medical discharge. Instead, the command ordered him tried for AWOL at a BCD Special Court martial, which could send him to prison for a year and give him a Bad Conduct Discharge—barring Eugene from all VA benefits, including mental health care.

Several groups, including VVAW, Citizen Soldier, and "The Different Drummer" internet café located outside Ft Drum, all mobilized political and legal support for Eugene. The first active duty chapter of the Iraq Veterans Against War (IVAW) was organized at Ft Drum during this period and they also came to his aid. A week before his court martial, justice finally prevailed when the command announced that they were dropping criminal charges and would discharge Eugene with a General Discharge under Honorable Conditions.

Seeking Medical Treatment from the VA: Eligibility

The VA no longer attempts to function as the "doctor of last resort" for veterans. With the influx of new patients needing costly and extensive treatment, the agency has erected new barriers to access for many veterans. Even combat veterans are given health care for only two years, beginning on their date of separation from the military. In 2003, the VA stopped enrolling non-service-connected veterans whose income is above poverty levels. There are currently legislative proposals to remove this bar, but at press time, monies sufficient to implement the change have not been appropriated.[11]

Disability Compensation

This is one of the VA's largest programs. If a veteran has a health problem which he or she believes was caused (or made worse) by military service, they can apply for recognition as a "service connected" disability. This is a two step process. First, the vet must establish that the health problem developed during service and second, that it has caused a measurable level of disability.

The VA's Liability for Medical Malpractice

Lawsuits for injury or death due to malpractice or incompetence at the VA medical facility cannot be filed as normal tort lawsuits in either federal or state courts. Instead, they must be filed under the Federal Tort Claims Act, which restricts the normal rights of plaintiffs. For example, all cases are heard by a federal judge sitting without a jury. Also, no punitive damages can be awarded, no matter how willful or egregious the misconduct of the VA employees.

Conclusion

Today, care at the VA health system is probably closer to that provided at many civilian medical centers than it was thirty years ago. However, this may be due less to improvements in the VA's system and more to the overall deterioration of healthcare in the civilian sector. Forty million Americans today who lack medical insurance often do not have access to preventative health care or prompt medical intervention. They are left to a patchwork of public-care providers and emergency rooms. This, predictably, leads to longer and more serious bouts of illness.

It is only when American society finally decides to commit the resources necessary to create a system of universal health care for every citizen, that our health systems, including that of the VA, will attain a level of care that citizens of other industrialized nations take for granted.

Further Reading

Anderson, Rick. *Home Front: The Government's War on Soldiers.* Clarity Press, 2004.

Cortright, David. *Soldiers in Revolt. Haymarket Press, 2006.* (A fascinating account of the "GI coffeehouse movement" which played a big part in ending the Vietnam war)

Ensign, Tod. *America's Military Today.* New Press, 2005. (An overview of the US military today, with an emphasis on the current wars in Iraq and Afghanistan)

Mejia, Camilo. *Road from Ar Ramadi.* New Press, 2007. (A personal memoir by the first Iraq vet to refuse further duty in Iraq)

Michel, Christopher P. *The Military Advantage.* Simon & Schuster Paperbacks, 2006.

Scahill, Jeremy. Blackwater: *The Rise of the World's Most Powerful Mercenary Army.* Nation Books, 2007.

8

ILLUSION

War boosts the economy for all Americans.

REALITY

**Wars benefit the rich, but the American standard
of living generally declines, with the poor paying the most.**

Jesu Estrada

Before the onset of the war in Iraq, President Bush asserted that
the war would be brief and the cost minimal, no more than $50 billion
dollars. Underlying this flawed estimate was the implication that the
American people would not be affected by Bush's crusade to promote
democracy and defeat terrorism. Now, even conservative analysts like
David Leonhardt, business columnist for the *New York Times*, have pointed
out that these initial estimates are so far off that the true cost of war could
reach the trillions. He argues:

> The deteriorating situation in Iraq has caused the initial
> prediction to be off the mark by a scale that is difficult to
> fathom. The operation itself—the helicopters, the tanks, the
> fuel needed to run them, the combat pay for enlisted troops,
> the salaries of reservists and contractors, the rebuilding of
> Iraq—is costing more than $300 million a day.[1]

The average American might have a difficult time imagining what
to do with 300 million dollars a day, but what is becoming clearer day by
day as social services are being decimated is that the expenditures of war
are affecting *everyone*. Most notably, the cost of war affects those people
at the bottom of the socio-economic ladder, although the middle class
manager and penny-pinching housewife are also finding it difficult to
make ends meet. This chapter looks at how the bottom sector of society
and social services are affected by the war in Iraq and explains the impact
on expenses to the general population.

Shortly after the war in Iraq, homeless shelters and food pantries began to close down as states funneled funds towards the war in Iraq. Most notably in Washington State, the governor, in an irrational effort to support Bush, closed a significant number of shelters, while the homeless population rose and children went underinsured both in medical and dental needs. The money for the war against "terror" has to come from somewhere. Unfortunately, that happens to be the pockets of the poor and most vulnerable in this country.

Military spending increases gap between rich and poor

Despite the bloodshed of both enemies and our military personnel, wars in the past served as a means to jumpstart the economy and create jobs. Most notably during World War II, because the economy was based on industry, war pulled America and much of the world out of the Great Depression, as many manufacturing and military jobs were created. The same was true during the Korean War and was seemingly the case during the Vietnam War. However, military efforts from the seventies on have not improved the economy, nor helped alleviate poverty.

Several studies in the early 1990s indicated that military spending increased both unemployment rates and poverty rates. An historical analysis spanning from 1959-1992 [2] led economist Errol Henderson to conclude that while military spending during wartime decreased poverty, aggregate military spending increased poverty. In his 1994 study, "Military Spending and Income Inequality," John D. Abell proved empirically that *increases in military spending [were] associated with a widening gap between the rich and the poor.*[3]

Although current studies need to be done to determine the economic impact of war on the poor and unemployed, employment and poverty rates have not improved as a result of the war in Iraq or Afghanistan. In fact, according to the government census bureau, from 2001 to 2005 the poverty rate rose consecutively, capping at 12.4% of the overall population in 2004, a significant increase from the 1990s.[4] In the main, since 1980, poverty increased in almost every single state,[5] thereby demonstrating that the increase in military spending has not benefited the economy, as it had in the past.

Today, we can expect more drastic results from military spending as social services are being decimated to balance the war budget. Yet the full effects of this military spending will not be seen immediately, although the poor are already affected today. Ewen MacAskill of *The Guardian* explains what the effects of Bush's 2007 war budget would be:

> The huge rise in military spending is paid for by a squeeze on domestic programmes, including $66[billion] in cuts over five

years to Medicare, the healthcare scheme of the elderly, and $12[billion] from the Medicaid healthcare scheme for the poor.[6]

In the future, these cuts in social services will be devastating, considering the present inadequacy of Medicare and Medicaid healthcare to the poor, and given the rising cost of prescriptions and hospitalization.

Another government program that is being decimated is Social Security. In 2003, the National Committee to Preserve Social Security and Medicare began to send newsletters urging people to advocate their legislators to preserve social security.[7] As a result of the 2007 military budget, Social Security and Medicare face a $138 billion dollar cut over the next ten years.[8] Although that estimate is now one quarter of what it was in 2003, the cuts affecting these two programs are critical to retirees and the growing number of poor. Also, within that particular 2007 budget proposal were reductions in payments to providers in the Medicare system and payment caps in medical expenditures. How would the elderly and retirees who are struggling to make ends meet acquire the additional money needed to supplement what Social Security and Medicare fail to provide? Since the military budget seems to be increasing year by year, where will the cuts to these services end? The 2008 budget cuts an additional $10 billion dollars. If these trends continue, despite all the government rhetoric that it will promote the security of citizens, Americans' real security will continue to deteriorate.

The effects on the poor might seem marginal and inconsequential to many who may presently be gainfully employed, but one has to consider what kind of society American military spending will foster. The human cost in this country is just as important as the cost abroad. Do Americans want a society where the gap between the rich and the poor will continue to expand in a country with frayed and disappearing social nets? Do Americans want a country where the elderly and retirees are cast aside to fend for themselves? Do we want to see starvation and masses of homeless living on the streets? These questions are critical and should be at the forefront of the national debate, as the discontentment increases over military failures, because they are central to the viability of the military option.

How the Cost of War Affects You

In May 2007, Kansas was accosted by a series of tornadoes. The National Guard was so understaffed and equipment so scant that the guard could not respond to people's needs. Senator Harry Reid of Nevada admonished the lack of resources, not in order to criticize the National Guard, but to point out a glaring fracture in national security. He said:

In the wake of the tragic tornadoes that ripped through Kansas this past weekend, our National Guard did a fantastic job, and we are grateful for their work. But the toll of the war in Iraq crippled the ability of our National Guard to do the dangerous and heroic jobs they are charged with doing.[9]

Kansas Governor Kathleen Sebelius elaborated: "Fifty percent of our trucks are gone. Our front loaders are gone. We are missing humvees that move people. We can't borrow them from other states because their equipment is gone. It's a huge issue for states across the country to respond to disasters like this."[10] Prior to Kansas, the woefully inadequate response to Katrina showed the lack of preparedness by the government, whether it concerned the time it took to rescue people, or delays in provision of basic necessities like medicine, food, and shelter. America is still feeling the effects of this disaster and the government's inability to meet the needs of devastated residents. These two case studies beg the question: Are the money and resources truly being spent to keep America safe?

In a biting criticism, author Barbara Ehrenrich asserted, "The proposition that our bloated national security apparatus has made us more secure is open to debate, if not to outright derision."[11] If the government is not prepared to respond to natural disasters, what would happen if a supposed terrorist attack were to occur in the U.S.? Although this proposition has been used to spread fear and paranoia on a global scale, most Americans don't need analysts to understand that the hatred towards Americans has increased exponentially since the invasion of Iraq. The likelihood of an attack in America is more feasible now than before the U.S. invaded Iraq. But despite the passage of laws like the Patriot Act that curtail our domestic freedoms and the creation of the Department of Homeland Security, the focus of resources is so centered on military efforts abroad that America isn't any safer now than it was in 2000.

And what is the average American paying for this new predicament? According to *Mother Jones*, about "$1.9 billion a week, or $275 million a day" on the War in Iraq.[12] Almost a half trillion dollars in total.[13]

In fact, corruption in Iraq alone costs $4 billion dollars a year and "8.8 billion the U.S. gave the Iraqi government cannot be accounted for." Given the current state of Iraqi civilians, it's doubtful that money ended up in the pockets of those in dire need of medical supplies, food, and water. Although all life is precious, whether American or Iraqi, in a morbid analysis the article also priced the cost of lost American soldiers and compensation to Iraqi families by the U.S. government:

[A] U.S. Army private killed in action, leaving a spouse with three kids, $500,000 plus $40,000 annually...[An] Iraqi family killed by American missile ... [u]p to $2,500 per person.

Although no amount of money could make up for the loss of a loved one, let alone the minute amount for an entire Iraqi family, there is something infinitely dark and ironic about how American money is used to compensate for needless death.

Further Reading

Alnasraw, Abbas. *The Economy of Iraq: Oil, Wars, Destruction of Development and Prospects, 1950-2010.* Greenwood Press. March 1, 1994.

Foster, John Bellamy. *Naked Imperialism: The U.S. Pursuit of Global Dominance.* May 2006.

Jamail, Dahr and Amy Goodman. *Beyond the Green Zone: Dispatches from an Unembedded Journalist in Occupied Iraq.* Haymarket Books. October 2007.

"Military Recruiting 2006." National Priorities Project, December 22, 2006.

"More Unequal: Aspects of Class in the United States." *Monthly Review Press.*

Pelton, Robert Young. *Licensed to Kill: Hired Guns in the War on Terror.* Three Rivers Press. August 2007.

Smith, Michael K. *Portraits of Empire.* Common Courage Press. September 1, 2002. ISBN-10: 1567512208.

Stephen, Andrew. "Bush's blue-collar war." *New Statesman*, January 22, 2007.

Zinn, Howard. *The Unraveling of the Bush Presidency.* Seven Stories Press. August 30, 2007. ISBN-10: 158322769.

9

ILLUSION
We always win.

REALITY

**America stalemated in Korea, lost in Vietnam,
and cannot win the wars in Iraq or Afghanistan.**

Vic Blazier

On May 10th, 2003, less than two months after the first combat units rumbled across the Kuwaiti border into Iraq, President George W. Bush donned a flight suit and delivered a speech from the deck of the aircraft carrier, USS Abraham Lincoln. In this now infamous speech, later dubbed the 'Mission Accomplished' speech, the beaming Commander-in-Chief proclaimed a halt to major combat operations in Iraq. America and its piecemeal coalition had succeeded in toppling the notorious Saddam regime. The world breathed a sigh of relief, seemingly casting aside all pre-war doubts regarding flimsy intelligence and weak rationale for an invasion. I, for one, as a member of the U.S. armed forces in Iraq, can recall thinking that maybe preemptive war IS tolerable. After all, the world now had one less dictator to stomach.

Four years after this speech, the situation in Iraq is deteriorating, maybe even spiraling out of control towards all-out civil war. The insurgency in Iraq is growing. Nation-building on the part of America has been ineffective—if indeed that was truly what we were trying to do. The U.S. military finds itself stretched excessively thin, with many members serving an unprecedented two and three tours of duty in Iraq. Casualty counts, both civilian and military, are on the rise. I saw first-hand the expensive but delicate military hardware grinding to a halt under the stress of combat in an unforgiving environment. America has poured vast sums of its fortune into Iraq. On the home front and throughout the world support for the war is waning. My own personal experience with this war tells me that the very people America purports to have liberated from Saddam Hussein now clamor for liberation from what they believe is an occupation by meddling Westerners.

81

America will have to confront some difficult choices. With the 2006 general election, it is clear that American voters have already voiced their opinion that efforts in Iraq are not working. It has become clear that America cannot win the war in Iraq and it is time for a change in course.

Historical Precedent

History may well be the best indicator when making predictions about the eventual outcome of the Iraq war. Historically, the United States has found exceptional difficulty in waging war against a foe that resorts to guerrilla warfare and unconventional tactics, which is undeniably now the case in Iraq. The Korean War ended in a stalemate despite American firebombing (with napalm) and its threats to use nuclear and chemical weapons.[1]

The inability of the U.S. to deal with unconventional warfare was particularly evident in the 10 year "police action" in Vietnam, where American conventional forces were pitted against a resourceful and determined guerrilla force.

America lost the war in Vietnam, but it was not because the pajama-clad communist guerrilla forces in the jungles and rice paddies of Southeast Asia held all the decisive advantages. As is true today in the Middle East, American combat troops of the 1960's and 1970's were better equipped, better trained, and enjoyed better support than the forces they opposed on the battlefield.

Evacuees are helped on board an American helicopter atop a Saigon building on April 24, 1974.

During the Vietnam years, America leveraged its super-power status, pouring vast portions of its ground forces, air assets, and naval might into the struggle, while the communists relied on a resilient ground force equipped with little more than Chinese AK-47 assault rifles, time-tested guerrilla warfare tactics, a knowledge of their own homeland territory, some determination, the will to win, and a belief in the justice of their cause. Where Iraq is concerned, this recipe has not changed.

On April 30, 1975, the South Vietnam capital of Saigon fell to the North Vietnamese, ending a decade-long struggle that claimed the lives of over 2 million Vietnamese and over 58 thousand Americans. In the end, a simple David, armed only with primitive tools of war, slew a modern day Goliath — a hulking beast built for war. If history is an indicator, Goliath is poised to fall once again.

Military Limitations

Militarily speaking, the United States has consistently won all the key battles in Iraq, but it seems difficult not to foresee that we are losing the war in the meantime. Many indicators point to a grand defeat. Most notably, the Pentagon appears to be struggling, both in terms of manpower and in financing the war.

National level decision makers, hoping to avoid the backlash that accompanied the Vietnam era draft, have forgone the use of conscripts, relying instead on the nation's relatively small volunteer force — quietly supplemented by an equal or larger force of mercenaries, well-paid or not, depending on their country of origin. The "grunts" of the Army and Marine Corps have been forced to endure most of the workload in Iraq, resulting in a seemingly never-ending rotation in and out of battle. I managed to leave the country unscathed, but many of our troops return home physically maimed and psychologically affected for the rest of their lives after just one deployment. The odds increase with multiple deployments — and believe me, the troops and their families know it.

The limited number of units military tacticians have available for rotation has also resulted in a heavy reliance on part-time Reserve and National Guard personnel, with many of them being called to active duty for two-year hitches. Educational standards and character requirements have been relaxed at recruiting stations throughout the country. Twenty thousand dollar enlistment bonuses are handed out like door prizes to anyone with a heartbeat who is willing to sign a contract for four years. Thousands of "volunteer" service members have been subjected to a mandatory stop-loss program with a view to keeping them in uniform far beyond their enlistment contract. I myself fell victim to this unfair practice, and was forced to remain in uniform some four months after my enlistment contract ended. I was one of the lucky ones — some have fared far worse. Finally, in recent months several Congress members and high-level policy makers have begun calling for a draft as a means of preventing a complete depletion of the volunteer force.

The signs of desperation in our war machine are easy to detect. The brass in the Pentagon has been busy trying to ensure a victory in Iraq with limited options. The quick fixes and temporary bandages will hurt America's military branches in the end while simultaneously draining the nation's coffers. Perhaps preservation of individual careers and the influence of the politics of war are more powerful forces than the realities of war, especially for civilian and high-ranking chess players in the Pentagon who pass their days without fear of being killed by a roadside bomb or succumbing to the extreme heat that many of us dreaded even more. Whatever the case, the course the Pentagon is on now will only result in prolonging the inevitable — that America cannot win in Iraq.

Those Who Know Say "No"

One does not have to look very hard to find qualified personalities who concede that a victory in Iraq is untenable. Henry Kissinger, former U.S. Secretary of State under President Richard Nixon, recently stated during a televised interview that a military win in Iraq is impossible:

> If you mean by 'military victory' an Iraqi government that can be established and whose writ runs across the whole country, that gets the civil war under control and sectarian violence under control in a time period that the political processes of the democracies will support, I don't believe that is possible.[2]

It should be noted that Kissinger's tenure as Secretary of State spanned the last two years of the Vietnam conflict, which raged from 1965 to 1975. Given his historical perspective, the point can be argued that perhaps no other living human being is more qualified to draw the conclusion that an American military solution in Iraq will not succeed.

Former foreign relations gurus are not the only ones sounding alarm bells. The current UN envoy to Iraq, Special Representative Ashraf Qazi, fears all-out civil war.[3] Citing the devastation caused by recent tandem car bombings in the Baghdad burrow of Sadr City which killed approximately 200 Iraqi civilians, he warned that "Iraq would continue to descend into a civil war situation and people would become the victims of an unprecedented human rights catastrophe."

None of these warnings have been wasted on those of us who have served. In fact, history will likely show that some of the first rumblings regarding America's dire consequences in Iraq have originated from those experiencing it first-hand. While deployed to Iraq in 2004, one "old and seasoned Non-Commissioned Officer with nearly 20 years under [his] belt"[4] offered his belief in an essay that America's preference for politics and wholesale refusal to accept the reality of the guerrilla war in Iraq runs parallel with Vietnam, and will ultimately cost us another victory. A sense of desperation is also evident in the fast-rising desertion rate in the U.S. Army in 2007.[5]

As of Sunday, November 26, 2006, America's military involvement in the small Middle East country of Iraq has carried on longer than the U.S. engagement in World War II,[6] a war that spanned the entire globe. The only other war that America lost was Vietnam—a localized guerrilla war, just like Iraq. If history is an indicator, America cannot win in Iraq.

Further Reading

Galbraith, Peter W. *The End of Iraq: How American Incompetence Created a War Without End*. Simon & Schuster, 2007.

Isikoff, Michael and Corn, David. *Hubris: The Inside Story of Spin, Scandal, and the Selling of the Iraq War*. Three Rivers Press, 2007.

Kolko, Gabriel, *The Age of War: The United States Confronts the World*, Lynne Rienner Publishers, 2006.

Ricks, Thomas E. Fiasco: *The American Military Adventure in Iraq*. Penguin, 2007.

Ruppert, Michael C. *Crossing the Rubicon: The Decline of the American Empire at the End of the Age of Oil*. New Society Publishers, 2004.

Woodward, Bob. S*tate of Denial: Bush at War, Part III*. Simon & Schuster, 2006.

Protesters against the notorious School of the Americas in Fort Benning, Georgia seek to shut down an institution that trains Latin American police, military and government in counter-insurgency and torture. November 18, 2007.

COMPASSION

We Do Not Mistreat the Enemy

Americans are spared the horrors of war by a media that refuses to show the damaged bodies and the devastation of the villages. To a great degree, we have accepted this. As T.S. Eliot once wrote, "Humankind cannot bear much reality."

As a result of being ill-informed, Americans generally do not feel that they've been affected by the war.[1] The International Committee of the Red Cross released its report "Civilians Without Protection: The ever-worsening humanitarian crisis in Iraq" in part because the international community seems to have become desensitized to the extent of human suffering caused by the war.[2]

This apparent tolerance of the carnage does not reflect a lack of compassion among Americans. We tolerate the destruction because the alternative would bring even greater destruction. Modern warfare, we are assured, is characterized by surgically precise bombings that target enemy military sites with pinpoint accuracy. Before the Iraqi War, Ted Koppel and Tom Brokaw both reminded their viewers that high-tech weapons are

Coalition soldiers walk behind humiliated Iraqi prisoners.

used to minimize civilian casualties.[3] George Bush told the people of Iraq, "If we must begin a military campaign, it will be directed against the lawless men who rule your country and not against you."[4] Even economic sanctions, which have victimized civilian populations to a far greater degree than anticipated, have been condoned by the American public because they seemed a better alternative to the bombings.

But as we learn the truth, and become more aware of the agonies suffered by the victims of our bombs and our sanctions, are we truly a compassionate people if we allow the devastation to continue?

10

ILLUSION
Suffering is minimized in today's wars.

REALITY

**The havoc wreaked upon civilian populations
is unparalleled, intended, and unmitigated.**

Kathy Kelly

In the spring of 2007, on a warm, breezy evening in Chicago, students from a United States Naval Academy high school band performed their first outdoor concert. An audience of several dozen people sat in folding chairs on the school lawn. On the sidewalk bordering the school, another group assembled, bearing placards urging "Courage for Peace, Not for War," and calling for an end to war in Iraq.

As band members tuned their instruments, several of the Naval Academy students approached the dozen or so people holding signs and banners. "Why are you disrespecting us?" asked one youngster. "Don't you understand that this school is helping us? They teach us discipline. If we were in a regular high school, people would be asking us to buy drugs and become gang-bangers."

An hour long conversation ensued. The students seemed convinced that if the U.S. didn't fight terrorists in Iraq, the terrorists would be in the United States; attacks like 9/11/2001 would occur regularly. Some mentioned that the U.S. had to fight in Iraq to prevent another Hitler.

I was holding a vinyl banner bearing an almost life-size image of Ali, a teenager in Iraq. "Who's he?" asked one of the students. I told them that I'd known Ali since he was seven years old, that his mother was a widow with nine children, and that their small apartment had recently been destroyed by a car bomb explosion. Including Ali in the conversation through picture and story opened up more of a dialogue. Students told about their own difficulties and hardships. One young woman's older brother had been killed at the local high school she'd be attending if she hadn't been accepted at the military academy. Another young man said that he travels all the way from the projects on the south side of Chicago to attend this school. He said he had no intention of joining the military, but that at least this was a way to get an education that would help him get out of the projects.

I told the students that 20 years ago, I had taught high school. The high school students whom I'd taught had dropped out or been expelled from local Chicago high schools. Three of the students had been killed each year that I taught in the alternative school. The Naval Academy students nodded attentively when I told them that I insisted students leave their writing in binders on our classroom shelves, knowing that if one of them died before the school year ended, I could at least offer a binder of their writing to the bereaved family. I told them that even now I shudder, remembering that in a particular folder, I had kept various graphics that could be used for hastily prepared programs at funeral liturgies.

We agreed that even a tiny fraction of the billions, even trillions of dollars spent on war in Iraq could pay for better education and social programs to benefit children in every neighborhood of Chicago.

"So, what did you do instead of teach?" asked one student. I replied that I'd gone to Iraq as often as possible, and that I'd tried to listen to many Iraqis, especially young ones close to him in age. The student shook his head, clearly puzzled. I would have liked to unfold a much longer story about what my companions and I, in the peace movement, have seen and heard during successive U.S. wars in Iraq.

My own awareness of the story began in August of 1990.

On August 2, 1990, Iraq had invaded Kuwait. Four days later, the United Nations began to enforce against Iraq the most comprehensive economic sanctions ever imposed in modern history. Saddam Hussein did not withdraw from Kuwait, and the United States began a massive military buildup for an eventual war against Iraq.

I knew that in reality the U.S. government was preparing to invade Iraq, not because it couldn't tolerate brutal dictators or illegal invasions: the U.S. had recently invaded Panama and before that, Grenada, and it was propping up numerous dictatorships around the world, many of them brutal international aggressors, and many of which, like Saddam Hussein's regime, the U.S. had helped install.

This planned war was to dominate and control Iraq's resources and gain greater geopolitical control in the region.

We in the Gulf Peace Team prepared our response, but nothing could prepare us for what we saw in Iraq.

In the course of the 1991 Desert Storm bombing, U.S. aircraft alone dropped 88,000 tons of explosives on Iraq, the equivalent of nearly five Hiroshima nuclear blasts. Seventy percent of the so-called "smart" bombs missed their intended targets, often falling instead on civilian dwellings, schools, churches, and mosques. But the 30 percent that blasted on target wiped out electrical plants and sewage treatment facilities. The U.S. had specifically targeted Iraq's civilian infrastructure—power, sewage, bridges, roads, communication—and the lifeline for Iraq's poorest people was systematically destroyed.[1]

When I returned to the United States, in August of 1991, friends told me that during the Gulf War, many bars were crowded with people who watched the war coverage on large screen televisions. "Rock Iraq!" patrons would roar, lifting their mugs when a bomb hit its target. "Slam Saddam! Say hello to Allah!"

An increasingly imperial attitude had become pervasive, along with the illusion that if the United States was militarily and economically powerful enough, it could create its own moral reality.

Just before leaving the United States, a reporter asked me if there were any alternatives to the impending Gulf War. "Yes," I said. "The U.S. could allow continued usage of UN economic sanctions to coerce Saddam's withdrawal from Kuwait."

Who could have known, then, how poorly informed I was? I had no idea how swiftly and devastatingly the economic sanctions would punish innocent Iraqis who had no control over their government.

However, crucial information was available to U.S. policy makers. Even though successive U.S. administrations claimed that the sanctions were intended only to contain Iraq and deter Saddam Hussein's regime from acquiring weapons of mass destruction, a 1991 report written by the United States Defense Intelligence Agency (DIA) explained that just six more months of economic sanctions could be expected to thoroughly degrade Iraq's water treatment systems.

The report, entitled "Iraq Water Treatment Vulnerabilities[2]," noted that Iraq's water treatment system was unreliable even before the United Nations sanctions. "With no domestic sources of water treatment, replacement parts and some essential chemicals, Iraq will continue attempts to circumvent United Nations Sanctions to import these vital commodities. Failing to secure supplies will result in a shortage of pure drinking water for much of the population. This could lead to increased incidences, if not epidemics, of disease."

The report also noted that Iraq's rivers "contain biological materials, pollutants, and are laden with bacteria. Unless the water is purified with chlorine, epidemics of such diseases as cholera, hepatitis, and typhoid could occur."

A Sixty Minutes reporter, Leslie Stahl, asked U.S. Ambassador to the United Nations Madeleine Albright, in May of 1996, if she believed the deaths of over one half million Iraqi children were an acceptable price to pay for the U.S. policy in Iraq. Ms. Albright responded, "Yes, Leslie, I'm a humanitarian person, and it's a difficult choice to make, but the price, we think the price is worth it."

The sanctions lasted for 13 years.

As a member of "Voices in the Wilderness," a campaign to end those sanctions, I traveled to Iraq over two dozen times between 1996 and 2003.

Here is an excerpt from a diary I kept in 1996:

It's August 10, 1996, a sweltering day in southern Iraq during one of the hottest summers on record. I sink onto my bed at the Basrah Towers Hotel, grateful for the fan overhead and the promise of slightly less intense heat as evening falls. I don't feel particularly tired, but my companions insisted I take a break because I fainted after visiting the Basrah Pediatrics and Gynecology Hospital.

Dr. Tarik Hasim Habeh, the young director of residents, had taken us through several children's wards. Infant after infant lay wasting and skeletal in squalid conditions. We saw children suffering severe malnutrition, respiratory diseases, leukemia, and kidney disease. In one room, 14 incubators were stacked against the wall, useless for lack of repair parts. The blood bank consisted of one miniature refrigerator and an ancient centrifuge.

Dr. Habeh explains that the hospital is chronically short-staffed. Doctors can't earn enough to feed their families, sometimes no more than $3 per month, so some work instead as taxi drivers, street vendors or waiters.

The temperature in Basrah today is 140 degrees. Under these conditions, one should drink at least a gallon of water a day. Because sanctions bar chlorine used for water purification, even most bottled water, for the few who can afford it, is contaminated. At the water ministry, officials showed us rusted pipe sections with large holes that allow contaminants to leak into Basrah's drinking water.

I reach for the bottled water that Father Kassab gave us. "Drink this," he said, "and mark your bottles. We call this sweet water, water from Baghdad. I can tell you that if you drink the other bottled water here it will make you very sick." I think of the desperately ill children I met earlier today, and put the bottle aside. And my thoughts return to Fr. Kassab.

Basrah is Iraq's third largest city. Before the long years of the Iran-Iraq war, the Gulf War and the six-year siege of sanctions, it was a thriving oil port. Now, of 300 families interviewed by Archbishop Kassab, only 45 have at least one working family member. Unwillingly idle, frustrated and humiliated, Basrans trudge through streets fouled with sewage and bordered with piles of human waste. The piles, five to six feet tall, are left to dry, spaced every thirty feet. Adults negotiate residential sidewalks with care, stepping over human feces, and wastewater spills from the streets into nearby homes.

Meanwhile, amidst it all, smiling children, totally innocent victims of the silent war, rush forth to pose for our cameras.

In our visits to Iraq from 1996-2003, we saw first hand the horrible consequences of the economic sanctions. Saddam Hussein may not have missed a meal; arguably his control over the country was strengthened while the sanctions battered the civilian population, brutally and lethally punishing Iraq's most vulnerable people, the elderly, the sick, the poor, and in a tragedy beyond words, hundreds of thousands of children. The 15-year economic siege devastated the economy, wrecked the infrastructure, prevented rehabilitating water purification systems, and debilitated health care systems. The economic sanctions were a monstrous crime against humanity, a silent weapon of ghastly, massive destruction.

In August of 1999, UNICEF Executive Director Carole Bellamy held a press conference to announce the release of a "Situation Analysis of Women and Children in Iraq,"[3] which carefully explained that the economic sanctions contributed to the "excess deaths" of over 500,000 Iraqi children under age five. Not one U.S. television network aired coverage of the press conference. Only two of 50 leading U.S. papers reported the actual shocking number of one half million "excess deaths" of children.

Now, in 2007, close to two million Iraqis are internally displaced, having fled violence in their neighborhoods; 750,000 Iraqis who fled violence in their country now live in Jordan. Hundreds of thousands of these people live in wretched conditions. Another 850,000 Iraqis have fled to Syria. The U.N. estimates that one out of every 10 Iraqis will try to flee their country in 2007.

Television coverage regularly shows blood-spattered streets and charred vehicles at the intersections where suicide bombers detonate their murderous cargo. Gruesome carnage and desperate bereavement are part of everyday footage filmed in Iraq. A growing humanitarian catastrophe is more difficult to portray.

Every family in Baghdad struggles with fuel and energy crises. They get one hour of electricity every 12 hours; only the more well-to-do families can afford a back-up generator. Fuel for transportation is extremely expensive. In a society that has 50% -75% unemployment, many find themselves scrounging for basic necessities.

Families that receive the dreaded knock on the door giving them 24 hours notice—leave or you will be killed—must swiftly relocate to other areas where they often face problems gaining access to food, potable water and health care.

There should be massive relief convoys traveling into Iraq on a regular basis. There should be, but there aren't. Instead, U.S. lawmakers are asked to pour hundreds of billions of dollars into emergency supplemental funding for ongoing wars in Iraq and Afghanistan.

Nobel economist Dr. Joseph Stiglitz calculates that the war in Iraq, if it continues another eight years, will ultimately cost the U.S. economy 2.2 trillion dollars. It's shocking to think of what we've lost in dedicating this expenditure to war, rather than to domestic and foreign aid which could save millions of lives lost to hunger and illness, or, say, to renewable energy development which might save hundreds of millions from economic and environmental disasters now clearly on the horizon. Who are the criminals?

Many people argue that the troops are needed to stabilize conditions in Iraq. When I hear earnest concerns for Iraqi civilians, I can't help but wonder why these concerns were so absent when economic sanctions against Iraq directly contributed to the deaths of hundreds of thousands of Iraqi children under age five. Have we now a new slogan? "No Iraqi child left behind?"

A May 8th, 2007 "Save the Children" report stated that in 2005 in Iraq, 122,000 children didn't reach their fifth birthdays. Conditions didn't improve in 2007. The World Health Organization reported that 80 percent of Iraqi families have home sewage facilities that contaminate their water sources, and 70 percent of families don't have regular access to clean water; as a result diarrhea and respiratory infections now account for two thirds of the deaths of children under age five. Twenty-one percent of Iraqi children are now chronically malnourished.[4]

The report also notes that 70 percent of Iraqis who die in hospitals after violent injuries would have survived if the hospitals were adequately equipped.

Anyone listening to Iraqis tell about experiences of loss and tragedy would surely understand feelings of cynicism, even bitterness, when many bereaved Iraqis think about how the Bush Administration views the ongoing war in their country.

When asked in January, 2007 if he owed the Iraqi people an apology for not doing a better job of providing security after the invasion, President Bush quickly deflected the responsibility to the Iraqis:

> I think I am proud of the efforts we did. We liberated that country from a tyrant. I think the Iraqi people owe the American people a huge debt of gratitude. That's the problem here in America. They wonder whether or not there is a gratitude level that's significant enough in Iraq.[5]

The U.S. could direct the amount of money spent on just six hours of the war in Iraq and fully meet the UN Refugee Agency request to assist millions of people who have barely survived this U.S. "war of choice."

Words to a poem, written by Turkish poet Nazim Hikmet and sung by Pete Seeger, come to mind, thinking of the Iraqi children who have not survived:

> I come and stand at every door
> But no one hears my silent tread
> I knock and yet remain unseen
> For I am dead, for I am dead.

Further Reading

Dellinger, David. *From Yale to Jail*. Pantheon, 1993.

Deming, Barbara. *We Are All Part of One Another*. New Society Publishers, 1984.

Ferri-Smith, David. *Battlefield Without Borders: Iraq Poems*. Haleys, 2007.

Ishiguro, Kazuo. *Never Let Me Go*. Vintage, 2006.

Ishiguro, Kazuo. *Remains of the Day*. Faber and Faber, 2005.

Ishiguro, Kazuo. *When We Were Orphans*. Faber and Faber, 2005.

11

ILLUSION

Our modern military warfare only kills the 'bad guys'.

As US bombs get smarter, civilian casualties increase.
And they don't bring us any closer to winning.

Marc Herold

"Bombs that Turn Our Leaders into Butchers"[1]
Simon Jenkins
The Times, January 17, 2001

A series of interconnected myths has been woven to justify the execution of post-Vietnam military interventions abroad by the United States. The idea of being able to wage an aerial precision war has been central to the post-Vietnam era.[2] Our technological prowess is alleged to now allow us to wage war with few civilian casualties (or minor "collateral damage"). Every effort will be expended by the American state to present and sell this precision myth.[3] The American corporate media is called upon to propagate it. The mainstream corporate media has been a faithful stenographer with a few notable exceptions.[4]

Precision war will allegedly help win hearts and minds by minimizing civilian anger.

My purpose here is to disentangle these myths and to counter-pose an alternative series of realities. My focus will be upon Afghanistan—the so-called good war—though the arguments presented have a more general salience.[5] American military intervention in Afghanistan was accomplished through the use of air power, with small highly mobile U.S. Special Forces units on the ground to guide the bombing, and the purchase of Northern Alliance military forces enabled a quick ouster of the Taliban with minimal U.S. casualties. The necessary legacy, however, has been yet another brutal, undemocratic and corrupt regime in Kabul and a military stalemate.

Advocates of precision-guided munitions point out that civilian death as a proportion of total war deaths have been declining. Their point is illustrated in Table 1.[6]

Table 1 Civilian and Military Casualties in Recent Wars

War:	Civilian deaths	Total deaths	Civilian deaths as % of total deaths
WWII, Russia	7,700,000	21,300,000	36 %
WWII, Germany	3,810,000	7,060,000	54 %
Korea, 1950-53	900,000	2,900,000	31 %
India-Pakistan, 1971	500,000	1,000,000	50 %
Franco-U.S. Vietnam 1945-54, 1963-73	1,300,000	2,700,000	48 %
Soviet-Afg. 1979-89	1,000,000	1,500,000	67 %
Serbia-Bosnia-Croatia, 1991-95	230,000	300,000	77 %
Iraq, 1991	15,000	135,000	11 %
Yugoslavia, 1999	1,200	3,500	34 %
US-Afg. 2001-2	3,600	13,600	26 %

However, Table 1 lists fatalities resulting from all causes and, therefore, is no indication of the relative lethality of air wars.

Certainly, abandoning the so-called area bombing or strategic bombing of earlier conflicts has reduced the civilian toll. But the four civil wars of the 70s-90s have been extremely deadly for civilians. What is missed in such facile comparisons is that while the tonnage dropped is much smaller in recent conflicts, the ratio of civilians killed per 10,000 tons dropped remains high.

In a brief empirical review of wars since the Napoleonic ones [1803-1815], Clemens and Singer argue that "modern warfare kills more civilians than soldiers."[7] The main reason is that post-WW II conflicts have begun as civil wars and have been waged on the ground. The International Peace Research Institute claims a ratio of 8 to 1 of civilian to combatant deaths. Robert Rhodes noted that by the 1970s, civilians accounted for 73% of war deaths, a figure which rose to 85% in the 1980s.[8]

However, the Afghanistan war departed sharply from such a trend. At least two reasons can be adduced: 1) the Afghan war has been dominated by U.S bombing and intra-group fighting has been quite minimal;[9] and 2) the Taliban, Pakistani volunteer and Al Qaeda forces invited major casualties by opting for positional warfare in the Shomali Plain and around Kunduz during Oct/November 2001.

While no estimates exist of Taliban and their allied forces' deaths, a safe guess would be between 8,000-10,000.[10] Hence, the ratio of military to civilian deaths would be about 3 to 1. For Iraq in 1991, on the other hand, U.S. military sources estimate 75-105,000 troops died and Iraqi sources supported by subsequent eyewitness accounts, estimate 7,000 civilians died in the aerial assault; the ratio being 12 to 1 (Table 2).[11]

The heavy use of cluster bombs in modern wars further contributes to elevated civilian casualties.[12] The high dud rates of cluster bombs turn them into indiscriminate weapons.[13]

Table 2 Casualties in Modern *Air* Wars

	Military deaths	Civilian deaths	Total deaths	Civilian deaths as % of total deaths
Iraq, 1991	75,000- 105,000- 120,000	3,000- 7,000- 15,000-	78,000- 135,000	4 - 11%
Yugosl., 1999	1,800- 2,000	1,200- 1,500	3,000- 3,500	34 - 50%
Afghanistan, 2001-2002	8,000- 10,000	3,100- 3,600	11,100- 13,600	23 - 33 %

No inference should be drawn here about modern aerial warfare being more "humane" in the sense of reverting back to the wars of the nineteenth century wherein mostly combatants died. As documented below, the air war in Afghanistan has been the costliest of four recent air wars in terms of civilians killed per tonnage dropped.[14] On the other hand, the daily intensity of the bombing [as measured in missions per day] has been far lower than in previous wars: the average missions per day figures are 1,500 for the Gulf War, 500 for Serbia, and only about 80 for Afghanistan.[15]

The declining numbers of sorties flows directly from increasing use of precision guided munitions [PGMs]. It is important to realize that, contrary to much official celebration of PGMs for having the ability to save civilian lives by targeting the military; *PGMs were not developed to save civilian lives*. Instead, the development of so-called precision weaponry has been driven by politico-economic considerations. Though expensive to develop with high initial fixed costs, the precision weaponry once deployed has relatively low variable costs. More importantly, using PGMs economizes greatly by requiring both fewer bombs and sorties to destroy a target. They are cheaper and permit less danger to pilots.[16]

The lingering hangover of Vietnam, with American troops returning to the shores here in body bags, has spurred military planners to develop ways of waging war with very few U.S. casualties. A war with few U.S. casualties can more easily be 'sold' or 'marketed' to the U.S. general public. All of this has dearly little to do with minimizing civilian casualties on 'the other side.' If PGMs do result in little perceived 'collateral damage,' that is a bonus in the politico-economic calculus. The widely disseminated public relations campaigns extolling the virtues of PGMs serve to allay human sensibilities of the U.S. general public, as well as the governments of moderate Arab and Islamic nations.

Stephen Budiansky, columnist and student of classified military affairs, has pointed out that the Afghan air campaign reflected an abandonment of the traditional theory of strategic bombing dominant from World War I up through the nuclear age, which stressed that air attacks should target the enemy's vital centers and in so doing undermine his will to fight.[17] The core concept was that a population's resolve would be sapped if enough government, urban and civilian infrastructure was destroyed. But history shows that rather than sapping resolve, such bombing strengthened resilience, seen most clearly in the Indo-Chinese air campaigns. And it has also been argued that Hitler's bombing of London and other areas strengthened rather than weakened Allied resolve.

Beginning with the Gulf War, a new view emerged which stressed hitting enemy *military forces directly*, assisted with the use of new precision weaponry, and *before* the launching of a ground war. The new precision weaponry basically economized on the amounts of munitions and numbers of sorties needed to destroy a target.[18]

The U.S. bombing campaigns around Mazar, Kunduz and Khanabad exemplify this approach.

Table 3 makes one stark point: PGMs have not decreased the ratio of civilians killed per 10,000 tons dropped. The past seven major U.S bombing campaigns fall into three clusters in terms of resulting civilian deaths. Allied air forces dropped more than 1.2 mn tons on Germany, killing 635,000 civilians during World War II, giving the largest ratio of 5,000 civilian deaths for every 10,000 tons dropped.[19] The Iraq Gulf War has the lowest ratio of civilians killed per tonnage dropped, though I am not suggesting it was a clean air war. The Vietnam and Serbian bombing campaigns are intermediate cases. Afghanistan fits into a third group with Cambodia and Laos. In each of these campaigns, PGMs or not, there were over 2,000 civilians killed for every 10,000 tons of bombs dropped. PGMs were absent during the campaigns against Cambodia and Laos, but featured in Afghanistan. Yet in every case the ratio of civilian deaths to 10,000 tons dropped was similar. In this context, it is rational to conclude that PGMs per se play no role in saving civilian lives.

Table 3 A History of U.S Bombing Campaigns and Resulting Civilian Deaths

Bombed region	Date	Tonnage dropped	Reported civilian deaths	Ratio civilians killed per 10,000 tons of bombs
Vietnam, Rolling Thunder campaign	1964-67	650,000	52,000 North Vietnamese	800
Laos	1965-73	2,000,000	350 - 500,000	1,750 - 2,500
Cambodia Arclight campaign	1969-73	540,000	50-150,000	926 - 2,778
Christmas bombing of Hanoi	1972	20,000	1,600	800
Iraq Gulf War	1991	88,000	2,500 - 3,200 7,000 - 15,000	284 - 363 - 795 - 1,705
NATO bombing of Yugoslavia	1999	13,000	500 - 1,200 -1,500	385 - 923 - 1,153
U.S Afghan War	2001	14,000	1,300 - 3,600	929 - 2,571
Iraq, March 20-April 5	2003	6,350	940-1,112	1,480 - 1,752

The above reveals that, in terms of civilian casualties, the *U.S. air wars of the past decade have gotten more and more costly [see rising kill ratios from Iraq to Yugoslavia to Afghanistan]. Where the campaign in Yugoslavia topped out at 1,153 per 10,000 tons, the Afghan was topped out at 2,571, yielding a new meaning to the term "precision."*[20]

The Afghan air war has been particularly destructive in terms of civilian impact deaths compared with previous aerial bombing campaigns, ranking alongside the devastation perpetrated upon Laos and Cambodia.[21]

A fundamental 'fact' about recent U.S. bombing campaigns is that as the *U.S. bombs get smarter, civilian casualties increase.* High levels of Afghan civilian casualties have been caused less from mechanical or human errors, malfunction, or faulty intelligence, and more because of *the decision by U.S. political and military planners to use powerful bombs in 'civilian-rich' areas where perceived military targets were located.*[22] As Professor Peter Spang Goodrich has pointed out, even when there are no mistakes PGMs cut a wide swath of blast, heat, and fragmentation, gouge huge craters, and wreak widespread havoc and destruction. The surgical prevision myth claimed by the Department of Defense implodes after the bomb explodes.[23]

Dropping bombs from high altitudes can lead to non-military persons and structures being hit, as admitted in *Aviation Week & Space Technology,*

> The problem in identifying targets from high altitude came into sharp focus last week when an F/A-18 dropped a 1,000-lb. laser-guided GBU-16 on a warehouse used by the International Committee of the Red Cross (ICRC) in northern Kabul, about 2 km from the city's airport.[24]

The advent of precision-guided munitions encouraged military planners to drop bombs on sites which previously might not have been hit for fear of causing widespread civilian deaths. In effect, PGMs may have also contributed to an irresponsible arrogance in accordance with the more reflexive fighting by U.S. soldiers.[25] But the main reason remains proximity to what these planners defined as military targets, which caused 3,100-3,600 Afghan civilian impact deaths,[26] or in equivalent U.S terms, 40-47,000 deaths.

No one denies that the accuracy of bombing has improved since World War II. For example, the circular error probability using a 2,000 pound unguided bombed dropped from medium altitude shows a marked improvement:

World War II	~1,000 meters
Korea	305 meters
Vietnam	122 meters
Afghanistan	30 meters

A common rule of thumb suggests a safe distance from a bomb is considered a meter for every pound of explosives—i.e., 500 meters for a 500 lb. Mark 82 bomb. Unlike the image of PGMs, cluster bombs are designed to carry out mass indiscriminate destruction, an extension of the massive killing in earlier air wars. Though cluster bombs were dropped to kill troops and destroy armor, they often fell into adjacent neighborhoods and fields—just as in Iraq later[27]—leaving a deadly legacy. Suzanne Goldenburg of *The Guardian* analyzed how "long after the raids, bomblets bring more death" across Afghanistan.[28]

Ghulam and Rabia Hazrat lived on the outskirts of Kabul near a Taliban military base. One day, a U.S missile landed in the family's courtyard and the neighborhood was showered with cluster bombs. Mrs. Hazrat remembers,

> There was no warning. I was in the kitchen making dough when I heard a big explosion. I came out and saw a big cloud of dust and saw my children lying on the ground. Two of them were dead and two died later in the hospital.[29]

The new excuse put out by the U.S and NATO militaries and their all too numerous civilian acolytes is that the Taliban are responsible for these civilian deaths because they hide in villages. Anyone vaguely familiar with the techniques of guerrilla warfare knows that resistance fighters mingle amongst the population. That population needs to be respected and served, as described in Mao's famous pamphlet *Serve the People*. The Algerian national liberation fighters fought the French in urban areas (as beautifully shown in the movie *The Battle of Algiers*). The Brazilian guerrilla leader, Carlos Marighela, wrote the famous *Mini-manual of Urban Guerrilla Warfare*.[30] Can anyone take seriously these claims by the U.S/ NATO militaries? What are we to expect—that the Taliban will congregate out in the open of the Helmand desert and fire RPGs at Apache attack helicopters or A-10 Warthogs or Canadian tanks?

In a comparative study of Afghan and Iraqi civilian deaths, I stated,

> Before dying in combat (or from an 'accident'),[31] a U.S. occupation soldier in Afghanistan will have participated in the killing of 16-19 Afghan civilians. Although data for Iraq is

not strictly comparable, the ratio of total civilian deaths to that of U.S. military deaths is 18.5-20.5. Another way of putting this is that civilians bear a rising and the overwhelming burden of modern war (so-called precision munitions notwithstanding).[32]

As I have argued elsewhere when using cost-adjusted data for weaponry, U.S. precision bombs are far more deadly than Taliban suicide bombs.[33]

The myth of precision warfare has been gradually exposed as the years have passed since the demise of the Taliban regime, though not because either the U.S. military has given up on managing the news or the mainstream corporate media has stopped serving as the Pentagon's stenographer.[34] The sheer scale of the civilian casualties could not be concealed in the electronic and digital era. The reliance of NATO upon air power and close air support bombing is contributing to further Afghan disillusionment and calls within NATO countries like Canada and Italy for a cessation of air strikes. Rome has called for the U.S. to end its military mission in Afghanistan over what it terms "morally unacceptable" civilian casualties.[35] Awareness in Britain is growing that British troops are losing the battle for "hearts and minds" because of rising civilian casualties and war damage.[36]

In August 2006, Mike Scheuer, who served as the chief of the bin Laden unit within the CIA's Counterterrorist Center during 1996-99, was asked about the situation in Afghanistan. His response was revealing:

> The President was sold a bill of goods by George Tenet and the CIA—that a few dozen intel guys, a few hundred Special Forces, and truckloads of money could win the day. What happened is what's happened ever since Alexander the Great, three centuries before Christ: the cities fell quickly, which we mistook for victory. Three years later, the Taliban has regrouped, and there's a strong insurgency. We paid a great price for demonizing the Taliban…They're remembered in Afghanistan for their harsh, theocratic rule, but remembered more for the security they provided. In the end, we'll lose and leave. The idea that we can control Afghanistan with 22,000 soldiers, most of whom are indifferent to the task, is far-fetched. The Soviets couldn't do it with 150,000 soldiers and utter brutality.[37]

Yet the future is perfectly clear: a repeat of Vietnam where local satrap forces do the ground fighting and the U.S/NATO provide massive, quick reaction aerial firepower—America's ace.[38] And after the destruction becomes too lengthy and horrific to be borne—withdrawal.

Further Reading

Biddle, Stephen D., "Allies, Airpower, and Modern Warfare: The Afghan Model in Afghanistan and Iraq," *International Security* 30, 3 Winter 2005-6: 161-176

Engelhardt, Tom, "Carnage from the Air and the Washington Consensus." TomDispatch.com, July 9, 2007.

Herold, Marc W., "A Dossier on Civilian Victims of United States' Aerial Bombing of Afghanistan: A Comprehensive Accounting [revised]." Cursor.org, March 2002.

Herold, Marc W., "Truth About Afghan Civilian Casualties Comes Only Through American Lenses for the U.S. Corporate Media (Our Modern-Day Didymus)," in Peter Phillips & Project Censored (ed), *Censored 2003. The Top 25 Censored Stories*. New York: Seven Stories Press, 2002: 265-294

Herold, Marc, "Archivistan file," Cursor.org <http://www.cursor.org/stories/archivistan.htm>.

Kolhatkar, Sonali and James Ingalls, *Bleeding Afghanistan: Washington, Warlords, and the Propaganda of Silence*. New York: Seven Stories Press, 2006, 304 pp.

Kolko, Gabriel, *Another Century of War?* New York: The Free Press, 2002, 165 pp.

Lambeth, Benjamin S., *The Transformation of American Air Power*. Ithaca: Cornell University Press and The Rand Corporation, 2000, 337 pp.

Lindqvist, Sven, *A History of Bombing*. New York: The New Press, 2000, 207 pp.

McKeogh, Colm, *Innocent Civilians. The Morality of Killing in War*. Basingstoke and New York: Palgrave, 2002, 200 pp.

Rockel, Stephen and Rick Halpern (eds), *'Collateral Damage': Civilian Casualties, War and Empire*. Toronto and London: Between the Lines Press and Pluto Press, forthcoming 2008.

12

ILLUSION
'Collateral damage' is an impersonal by-product of war

REALITY
**'Collateral damage' includes and disguises
the destruction of people.**

Gayle Brandeis

When I was young, my mom once forgot her wallet when she took me and my sister out to dinner. The owner made my mom leave us at the restaurant as "collateral" while she drove home to get her credit cards. I think of that now when I hear the term "collateral damage", of two little girls sitting in the stuffy coat check room, feeling scared and vulnerable, waiting for our mom to come save us. And I know the fear we felt, the vulnerability we felt, was nothing compared to what people in a war zone feel when bombs are raining down over their homes, over the places where they usually feel safe.

The Bush administration may say that suffering is minimized through modern warfare, they may be able to brush off "collateral damage" as an impersonal, inconsequential, byproduct of war, but that's because the suffering isn't visible. We aren't seeing many images of true pain, of true suffering, even though it's happening every day, in both Iraq and for the US troops who return home wounded in the dead of the night.

This is why I am so moved by our "Walk in Their Shoes" campaign at CODEPINK: Women for Peace.[1] This national campaign was inspired by the actions of CODEPINK New York, who set over one hundred pairs of children's shoes, each standing for a particular Iraqi child killed during the current war, in front of Hillary Clinton's Manhattan office. The powerful visual display—which of course represents only a tiny percentage of actual civilian deaths in Iraq—forced passers-by (and hopefully Hillary herself) to confront the true human cost of war.

Since then, we have staged Walk in Their Shoes actions throughout the country. Passers-by are often moved to donate hundreds of pairs of shoes, to label each pair with the name and age of a woman or

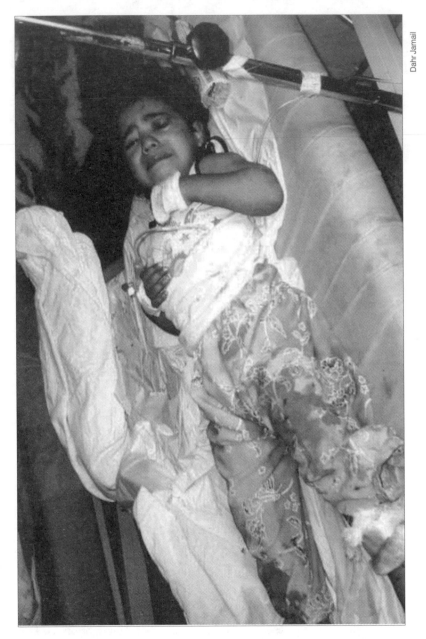

Dahr Jamail

Photo of wounded girl in Falluja. "Falluja used to be a modern city; now there is nothing." [Iraqi journalist, Ali Fadhil, cited in "Film reveals true destruction to ghost city Falluja," by Rory McCarthy, *Guardian*, Jan. 11, 2005.]

child killed in Iraq, to bear witness to the unspeakable pain this war has unleashed on the Iraqi people.

It is easy for politicians and media outlets to portray Iraqi casualties as numbers on a page, as faceless, nameless "collateral damage," far removed from any real pain. But when you see a worn pair of shoes, you can't help but think of the feet that once pulsed inside. The body connected to those feet. The heart and mind and voice connected to that body. The person's whole rich and complicated life, now silenced. You wonder if that person had blisters, or chipped nail polish, or pinched toes; you wonder if their soles ached, if they danced, if they ran through grass barefoot. If their feet were ever clasped in a gesture of love. You wonder about the fear they must have felt when the bombs started to fall. You wonder if they tried to outrun the destruction. You wonder about the pain that ripped through them when their flesh was pierced by shrapnel, when the walls began to fall. You wonder about the unbearable grief the surviving family members grapple with still. You wonder how we ever could have started such a tragic and unnecessary war.

In our effort to stop the next war now, we have been asking CODEPINK members to download photos of Iranian children and wear them as pendants with the message "Don't Bomb Iran." We want these images to remind our friends and neighbors and lawmakers of the humanity of the Iranian people. When we see the beautiful faces of these children, how could we ever come to terms with them as potential collateral damage? How could we ever risk harming such precious young lives?

We need to keep the human cost of war visible; we can't give our elected officials the luxury of looking away, of pretending that we are waging a humane and compassionate war.

Further Reading

Anderson, Sally and Hamill, Sam, Editors. *Poets Against the War.* Thunder's Mouth Press / Nation Books, 2003.

Benjamin, Medea and Evans, Jodie, Editors. *Stop the Next War Now: Effective Responses to Violence and Terrorism.* Inner Ocean Publishing, 2005.

Mason, Alane; Felman, Dedi; Schnee, Samantha (Editors). *Literature from the "Axis of Evil", A Words Without Borders Anthology.* New Press, 2006.

Pipher, Mary. *Writing to Change the World.* Riverhead Trade, 2007.

Rettig, Hillary. *The Lifelong Activist: How to Change the World Without Losing Your Way.* Lantern Books, 2006.

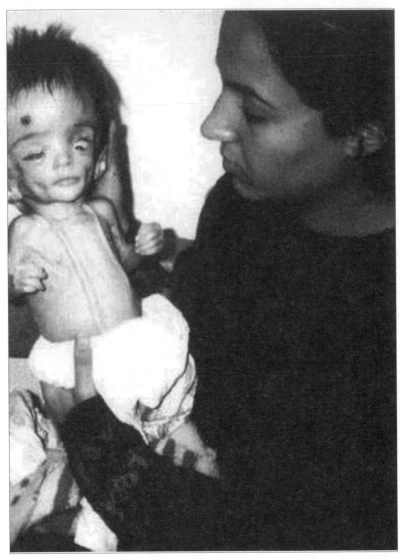

"Depleted" uranium weaponry, cluster bombs, and fuel air bombs have been declared to be in violation of international law by the United Nations experts sitting on the UN Sub-Commission on the Protection and Promotion of Human Rights. Reports and studies from the UN Secretary General and the Sub-Commission followed reports of high levels of cancers and birth defects after the introduction in 1991 of "depleted" uranium weapons by the US and UK during the first Gulf War.

13

ILLUSION
War is temporary.

REALITY
**Because of radiation, the effects of war
last many years beyond the end of fighting.**

Sherwood Ross

By firing radioactive ammunition, the U.S. and Great Britain may have triggered a nuclear holocaust in the Middle East that, over time, will prove deadlier than the U.S. atomic bombing of Japan.

While it is not possible to predict the future of a toxic epidemic with anything approaching certainty, emerging evidence that is both anecdotal and scientific indicates that the "depleted uranium" (DU) used in the Pentagon's armor-piercing munitions is a carcinogenic killer and a crippler; that it is indiscriminate, spreading its wings of death far and wide, inflicting dreadful agonies on civilian populations, particularly children, as well as troops in the field; and that some of its gruesome outcomes are already visible.

DU in Iraq

Christian Scherrer, a researcher at the Hiroshima Peace Institute, wrote in 2003: "Based on the report of the 48th meeting issued by the UN Committee dealing with the effects of Atomic radiation on 20th April 1999, noting the rapid increase in mortality caused by DU between 1991 and 1997, the IAEA document predicted the death of a half million Iraqis, noting that... 'some 700-800 tons of depleted uranium was used in bombing the military zones south of Iraq. Such a quantity has a radiation effect, sufficient to cause 500,000 cases which may lead to death.'"[1]

The Pentagon, however, has put the tonnage of DU fired by U.S. and U.K. forces at far less, 320 tons.

Scherrer points out that in 1991, DU ammunition was used mainly against Iraqi tanks in the desert near Basra but in the current conflict DU "is being used all over Iraq, even in densely populated areas including the heart of Baghdad, Mosul, Tikrit and other cities." Based on IAEA estimates and his previous research, he wrote, "the death toll may surpass a million deaths over the next few years, with more to follow!"

Scherrer noted that oncologist Jawad Al-Ali of Basra Hospital and Professor Husam al-Jarmokly of Baghdad University "showed a rapidly increasing death toll in Iraq since 1991 due to cancer and leukemia caused by U.S. radiological warfare." He based this on their December 1, 2002 presentation at the Peace Memorial Hall in Hiroshima. Al-Ali, a member of England's Royal Society of Physicians, told CounterPunch, "The desert dust carries death. Our studies indicate more than 40% of the population around Basra will get cancer. We are living through another Hiroshima."[2] Basra is a city of 1.7 million. Indeed, a *Christian Science Monitor* reporter who used a Geiger counter in August, 2003, found radiation readings between 1,000 and 1,900 times normal where fighting raged near Baghdad.[3]

Uranium is a heavy metal that enters the body via inhalation into the lung or via ingestion into the GI tract. It is excreted by the kidney, where, if the dose is high enough, it can induce renal failure or kidney cancer. It also lodges in the bones where it causes bone cancer and leukemia, and it is excreted in the semen, where it mutates genes in the sperm, leading to birth deformities. It has a half-life of 4.5 billion years.

Dr. Helen Caldicott, the prominent anti-nuclear crusader, has written: "Much of the DU is in cities such as Baghdad, where half the population of 5 million people are children who played in the burned-out tanks and on the sandy, dusty ground. Children are 10 to 20 times more susceptible to the carcinogenic effects of radiation than adults. My pediatric colleagues in Basra, where this ordnance was used in 1991, report a sevenfold increase in childhood cancer and a sevenfold increase in gross congenital abnormalities."[4]

Caldicott goes on to say the two Gulf wars "have been nuclear wars because they have scattered nuclear material across the land, and people — particularly children — are condemned to die of malignancy and congenital disease essentially for eternity." Because of the extremely long half-life of uranium 238, one of the radioactive elements in the shells fired, "the food, the air, and the water in the cradle of civilization have been forever contaminated."

Dr. Keith Baverstock, a World Health Organization radiation advisor, informed the media through a repressed WHO document that Iraq's arid climate would increase exposure from its tiny particles as they are blown about and inhaled by the civilian population for years to come.[5]

Doctor Zenad Mohammed, of the Basra teaching hospital maternity department, said that in the three months beginning in August, 1998 ten babies were born with no heads, eight with abnormally large heads and six with deformed limbs.[6] And the British *Guardian* newspaper reported Basra maternity cancer cases shot up from 80 in 1990 to 380 in 1997. The Guardian quotes gynecologist Basma Al Asam at Al Manoon hospital, Baghdad: "I've been watching this for seven years now and it's increasing. We're not just seeing babies born with congenital abnormalities, but very late spontaneous abortions because of congenital defects. In the past we used to see, maybe, one a month. Now it's two or three cases per day."[7]

According to Arthur Bernklau, of Veterans For Constitutional Law, of Port Jefferson, N.Y., "The long-term effect of DU is a virtual death sentence. Iraq is a toxic wasteland. Anyone who is there stands a good chance of coming down with cancer and leukemia. In Iraq, the birth rate of mutations is totally out of control."[8]

While such views are "anecdotal," the pain of the victims of DU is real and has been scientifically monitored. The *New Scientist* reported as far back as April 15, 2003,[9] "researchers at the Bremen Institute for Prevention Research, Social Medicine and Epidemiology in Germany have found that all is not well with the veterans. Last month they published results from tests in which they took blood samples from 16 soldiers, and counted the number of chromosomes in which broken strands of DNA had been incorrectly repaired. In veterans, these abnormalities occurred at five times the rate as in a control group of 40 healthy volunteers.[10] 'Increased chromosomal aberrations are associated with an increased incidence of cancers,' says team member Heike Schröder. The damage occurred, they say, because the soldiers inhaled DU particles in battle."

DU's Effect on Veterans

Doug Rokke, formerly the top U.S. Army DU clean-up officer and now anti-DU crusader, says he is quite ill from the effects of DU and that members of his clean-up crew have died from it. He also claims Israeli tankers fired radioactive shells during their invasion of Lebanon last year. U.S. and NATO forces are also said to have used DU ammunition in Kosovo.[11]

Colonel Asaf Durakovic, former nuclear medicine chief at the Wilmington, Del., VA hospital, said he found uranium isotopes in the bodies of Persian Gulf War veterans. *The New York Times* reported on January 29, 2001[12] that Durakovic found "depleted uranium, including uranium 236, in 62 percent of the sick gulf war veterans he examined. He believes that particles lodged in their bodies and may be the cause of their illness." Once inhaled, Durakovic said, "uranium can get into the bloodstream, be carried to bone, lymph nodes, lungs or kidneys, lodge there, and cause damage when it emits low-level radiation over a long period." *The Times* also called attention to the cancer deaths of 24 European peacekeeper soldiers in the Balkans "and the illnesses reported by many others."

Mutations akin to those associated with radiation poisoning have been reported among infants born to U.S. service personnel that fought in the Gulf Wars. One survey of 251 returned Gulf War veterans from Mississippi made by the Veterans Administration found 67% of children born to them suffered from "severe illnesses and deformities."[13] Some were born without brains or vital organs or with no hands or arms, or with hands attached to their shoulders. While U.S. officials deny DU ammunition is dangerous, it is a fact that Gulf War veterans were the first Americans ever to fight on a radioactive battlefield, and their children apparently are the first known to display these ghastly deformities.

Soldiers who survived being hit by radioactive ammunition, as well as those who fired it, are falling ill, often showing signs of radiation sickness. Of the 700,000 U.S. veterans of the first Gulf War, more than 240,000 are on permanent medical disability and 11,000 are dead, published reports indicate.[14] Their Gulf War Syndrome, denied by the Pentagon, has been commonly chalked up to a number of other factors, a literal "cocktail" of causes other than DU, such as vaccinations, possible exposure to germ warfare, oil well fires, and the like. Rokke and other Pentagon critics, though, believe a large portion of those who fell ill and/or died suffered from exposure to irradiated ammunition and that the Pentagon has engaged in covering up both the amount of DU expended and some VA medical records to prove it.

"Depleted uranium munitions were and remain another causative factor behind Gulf War Syndrome(GWS)," writes Francis Boyle, a leading American authority on international law in his book *Biowarfare and Terrorism*.[15] "The Pentagon continues to deny that there is such a medical phenomenon categorized as GWS—even beyond the point where everyone knows that denial is pure propaganda and disinformation," Boyle writes. He said the use of DU is outlawed under the 1925 Geneva Convention prohibiting poison gas, and contends that "The Pentagon will never own up to the legal, economic, tortious, political, and criminal consequences of admitting the existence of GWS. So U.S. and U.K. veterans of Gulf War I as well as their afterborn children will continue to suffer and die. The same will prove true for U.S. veterans of Bush Jr.'s Gulf War II as well as their afterborn children."

Conclusion

Chalmers Johnson, president of the Japan Policy Research Institute, writes in his *The Sorrows of Empire*[16] that, given the abnormal clusters of childhood cancers and deformities in Iraq as well as Kosovo, the evidence points "toward a significant role for DU." By insisting on its use, Johnson adds, "the military is deliberately flouting a 1996 United Nations resolution that classifies DU ammunition as an illegal weapon of mass destruction."

American Wars: Illusions and Realities / edited by Paul Buchheit

The civilian death toll from the August, 1945, U.S. atomic bombings of Hiroshima and Nagasaki has been the subject of some debate. It has been put as high as 140,000 and 80,000, respectively. Over time, however, deaths from radiation sickness are thought to have claimed the lives of many thousands more. The atomic bombings of Japan affected basically two cities, neither of which had populations remotely as large as Baghdad today. The attacks on Japan were confined to two small geographic areas. By contrast, in Iraq and Afghanistan, the irradiated ammunition has been fired indiscriminately.

While no one can predict with any certainty what the long-term outcome will be, the classic symptoms of radiation poisoning that are beginning to appear in the Middle East and the Balkans as cited by the above authorities, and others, must be taken with utmost seriousness. The war-makers apparently have made a good start on the road to holocaust.

Further Reading

Miller, Alexandra C. (Editor). *Depleted Uranium: Properties, Uses, and Health Consequences*. CRC Press, 2006.

Gut, Anne and Bruno, Vitale. *Depleted Uranium—Deadly, Dangerous and Indiscriminate*. Coronet Books, 2003.

Caldicott, Helen. *Poison Dust* (DVD). 2006.

Catalinotto, John and Flounders, Sara. *Metal of Dishonor—Depleted Uranium: How the Pentagon Radiates Soldiers & Civilians with DU Weapons*. International Action Center, 2004.

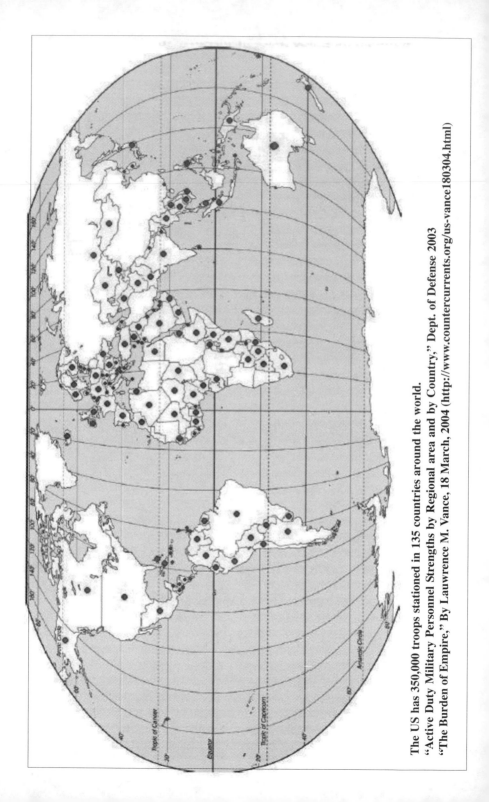

The US has 350,000 troops stationed in 135 countries around the world.
"Active Duty Military Personnel Strengths by Regional area and by Country," Dept. of Defense 2003
"The Burden of Empire," By Lauwrence M. Vance, 18 March, 2004 (http://www.countercurrents.org/us-vance180304.html)

ALTRUISM

We Are Making the World a Better Place

> *Every gun that is made, every warship launched,*
> *every rocket fired signifies, in the final sense,*
> *a theft from those who hunger and are not fed,*
> *those who are cold and not clothed.*
> — Dwight D. Eisenhower

We distribute our weapons and our wars and our beliefs throughout the world, convinced that we are promoting democracy and American values, secure in our belief that history will record the benefits of our altruism, and unwilling to be swayed by opinions to the contrary. We feel we are driven not only by self-interest, but also by the conviction that what is good for America will be good for others as well. We desire to share our good fortune with people in developing countries. Eventually, we believe, our actions will mean peace and prosperity for all of us.

But is this really true? A World Public Opinion poll shows that almost 3/4 of the world disapproves of our intervention in Iraq.[1] A recent Pew Survey shows "global distrust of U.S. leadership."[2]

Perhaps we Americans and our government, if we fail to acknowledge the opinions and feelings of those affected by our interventions, are not the altruists we aspire to be.

Futenma-Henoko Action Network

Okinawa: Some of the 35,000 who gathered in Ginowan City on March 5, 2006 to protest against latest base construction plans in Henoko and Oura Bays. If carried out, the plans will allow US forces to fulfil a long envisaged strategy to upgrade their military facilities.

Prague, Czech Republic, May 26, 2007. Thousands of protesters gathered in Prague during demonstration against planned US radar base in the Czech Republic.

Vicenza, Italy, February 17, 2007. More than 100 000 Protestors demonstrate against the expansion of a U.S. military base.

South Korea, September 24, 2006. The 4th Great Peace March to "oppose the Pyeongtaek US base expansion". U.S. troops have occupied Korean territory since 1953.

Iraq, April 22, 2003. Protests by the majority Shiite population. Banners say "IRAQ FOR IRAQIS" and "THANK YOU AMERICA. NOW GO HOME."

The wall seen here as it cuts through Jerusalem.
It is 25 feet high, twice the size of the Berlin Wall.

The U.S. has long provided diplomatic cover for Israel at the UN, in particular using its veto to shield Israel from condemnation by the Security Council.* When the World Court ruled (14-1) that Israel must cease construction on a wall separating Israel from the Palestinians, dismantle it, and compensate those affected, a subsequent General Assembly Resolution called on Israel to respect the World Court ruling. This resolution passed by 150 votes to 6, with only the United States, Israel, Australia, Micronesia, Marshall Islands and Palau voting against it. It typified the diplomatic isolation the U.S. is prepared to endure on Israel's behalf.

*For a list of US vetoes at the UN protecting Israel, see http://www.jewishvirtuallibrary.org/jsource/UN/usvetoes.html).

14

ILLUSION

*America's relationship with Israel promotes stability
in the Middle East*

REALITY

**The US-Israeli alliance has led to years of unrest
and human suffering in the Middle East**

Ghada Talhami

The history of US involvement in the Israeli-Palestine conflict goes back to the origin of the Arab-Israeli conflict when the UN partitioned Palestine into two states, one Jewish, which emerged as the new state of Israel, and one Arab, which was never realized. American complicity in leading up to this development goes beyond its support for a resolution which granted the one-third Jewish population, which at the time owned only 6% of the total land mass of Palestine, one half of its land area.

It is estimated that since 1949, the US has bestowed on Israel at least $51.3 billion in military subsidies, which is the largest amount of aid given to any other country during that period. Loans for military equipment to the Jewish state have amounted so far to $11.2 billion, in addition to the total sum of $31 billion in economic assistance and major loan guarantees for joint US-Israeli military projects. Gabriel Kolko, a foremost authority on modern warfare, explains that since 74% of these military grants are expected to remain within the US for purchasing American-made weapons, the grants have often resulted in the creation of jobs in many congressional districts. This led to the congressional tendency to heed appeals by the Israel lobby to support any demands for American military and economic aid.

The link between US and Israel military planning and weaponry encouraged Israeli generals to mimic recent American Middle East campaigns of "shock and awe," to disastrous results. The most glaring example of this was the manner in which the former Chief of Staff of the IDF, Dan Halutz, planned the war on Lebanon in the summer of 2006. This war, which was strategized in November of 2002, long before the "expected" kidnapping of two Israeli soldiers, was apparently fought and lost in the same style as recent US campaigns in Afghanistan and Iraq, and "mimicked" the shock and awe aspects of the American campaigns.[1]

What motivates the US to tolerate Israel's continued onslaught on the Palestinians in the West Bank and Gaza, leading it to stage military incursions into neighboring Arab countries? Now that the Cold War has ended, what arguments do the neo-conservatives and advocates of militarized, pre-emptive policies utilize in order to explain continued unlimited US support for the state of Israel? A recent study by John Mearsheimer and Stephen Walt has finally documented and demonstrated the extent of the impact of the pro-Israel lobby on US Middle East policy. The study questions the justification for this economic generosity towards a state which is by now neither poor, nor militarily vulnerable. Indeed, they argue, Israel enjoys a standard of living and high cost of labor comparable only to Western Europe.[2]

A further source of constant amazement is the degree to which the United States tolerates Israeli infringement of international law, as well as the naïve belief in America's immunity to international criticism as a result of this policy. Israel's first invasion of neighboring Lebanon in 1982, for instance, has generated severe criticism of the US since its adoption of the 1947 Geneva Conventions obligated it to seek Geneva Conventions compliance by its own allies. The US was considered particularly responsible since it supplied Israel with weapons and munitions.[3] US tolerance of Israel's egregious infringement of human rights law in the Occupied Territories in recent years has also caused an erosion of its status in the world.

George Bush's 2004 exemption for the large settlements, or "population centers," as he has recently referred to them,[4] means that Israel now has US consent to annex 85% of Palestinian lands. The Palestinians are expected to become willing participants in their own massive land alienation. Israel is also expected to seek to convert the Wall, or Separation Barrier, which it has built in order to enclose the settlements and the area of Greater Jerusalem within the territory of the Israeli state, into its new provisional borders. This would add an additional 10% to its land seizures. All of these developments will be irreversible given the current constellation of powers in Washington: support for Israel in both houses of Congress, a neo-conservative administration, the growing camp of the Christian Right, the Israel lobby, and military lobbyists who have long benefited from US economic and military aid for Israel.[5]

One of the most dangerous outcomes of the US-Israeli alliance has been America's historic support for and tacit approval of Israel's nuclear program. The ramifications of this policy are enormous and can be considered today as the main cause of the current Iranian challenge to Israel's nuclear hegemony in the region. The history of Israel's nuclear bomb dates back to the 1950s. Today, occasional official slips of the tongue on the part of people like Robert Gates and Ehud Olmert make it clear that Israel's reputed possession of more than 400 nuclear warheads and the ability to deliver them is more than just an open and unacknowledged secret.

It is not difficult to see how the American determination to anoint Israel as its Middle East surrogate and the area's unchallenged nuclear power have alienated radical and conservative Arab public opinion alike. Despite all claims to the contrary, even the most traditional Arab states in the area are unable to overlook the human cost of Israel's occupation of Palestinian lands and its detrimental effect on the legitimacy of their own regimes. The Organization of the Islamic Conference (OIC), an association of 57 states founded in 1969, represents a large segment of the world's population and one of its richest blocks of states.[6] As an expression of its support for the Palestinians' legitimate right of struggle against Israel's occupation regime, the OIC stated the following in a 2004 report to the UN:

> ...(we) distinctly distinguish acts of terrorism from the legitimate struggle of peoples under colonial or alien domination and foreign occupation for self-determination and national liberation—a right acknowledged under international law and resolutions of the UN.[7]

US and Israeli resistance to the idea of an independent Palestinian state continues to stoke the fires of Palestinian armed resistance and anti-American sentiment even on the part of friendly Arab allies. Israel's nuclear hegemony continues to aggravate the serious strategic imbalance in the Middle East. One of the main reasons for this dangerous picture is Israel's overwhelming emphasis on its own territorial security and the concomitant denial of the validity of Palestinian human and national rights. Despite its maximalist position, Israel continues to receive total backing from the US, which has not addressed Palestinian humanitarian and national needs. The US cannot proceed as though its pro-Israel policies hardly face any serious regional or international challenges.

Further Reading

Aronson, Shlomo. *Israel's Nuclear Programme, the Six Day War and its Ramifications.* King's College, London's Mediterranean Studies, n.d.

American Wars: Illusions and Realities / edited by Paul Buchheit

Boyle, Francis A.. *Palestine, Palestinians and International Law.* Clarity
    Press, Inc., 2003.
Farsoun, Samih K., and Naseer H. Aruri. *Palestine and the Palestinians.*
    Boulder, CO: Westview Press, 2006.
Lederman, Jim. *Battle Lines: The American Media and the Intifada.*
    Boulder, CO: Westview Press, 1992.
Mansour, Camille. *Beyond Alliance: Israel in US Foreign Policy.* New
    York: Columbia University Press, 1994.
Mearsheimer, John, and Stephen Walt. "The Israel Lobby." *The London
    Review of Books*, March 23, 2006.
Peri, Yoram. *Generals in the Cabinet Room: How the Military Shapes
    Israeli Policy.* Herndon, VA: Institute of Peace Press, 2006.

15

ILLUSION

*Developing countries ultimately benefit from
our wars for democracy.*

REALITY

**The Democratic Republic of the Congo
has suffered years of turmoil form our warlike behavior.**

Maurice Carney

Wherever conflict or war breaks out, one can be relatively certain that a group of elites will benefit in one form or another while the masses of the people suffer and die. When conflict or war occurs on the African continent, one does not have to dig too deep to find an imperial power behind the scene either pulling the strings or with the ability to influence one of its client states. These wars are almost always presented to the world as tribal conflicts, replete with wanton killing by bloodthirsty Africans on the so-called "dark continent." A cursory look will clearly demonstrate to the casual observer that this rendition of conflict on the African continent is far from the truth. What is almost always true is that these wars are universally about natural resources and there is usually a Great Power manipulating events in order to benefit from the enormous amount of natural resources that the African continent boasts. The United States, the greatest of the Great powers, has been a primary player and beneficiary as a result of conflict on the African continent.

Patrice Lumumba, the Democratic Republic of the Congo's first democratically elected Prime Minister, was assassinated on January 17, 1961. Lumumba's nationalist and pan-Africanist stance, arguing that the Congo's wealth belonged to the Congolese people, virtually assured his demise. The Americans and Belgians in particular but also the English and French were not about to allow the Congo prize with its vast natural wealth to be controlled by the Congolese, least of all a nationalist like Lumumba.

The neo-colonial era in the Congo was characterized by its client relationship with the West. The West, led by Belgium and the United

States, liquidated a democratically elected leader with the assistance of their Congolese sycophants, mainly Joseph Mobutu and Moise Tshombe. The United States played a key role in installing and maintaining Mobutu in power for over three decades, during which time the West had unfettered access to Congo's gold, diamonds, copper, cobalt, uranium and myriad other minerals central to the technological and military industry of the West.

The US-installed Mobutu was overthrown in 1997 and a new sheriff was in town, backed by Congo's neighbors, mainly Rwanda, with the blessing and backing of the United States[1] and strong support from the mining companies who struck deals with Laurent Desire Kabila while he was in the bush marching on Kinshasa.

Kabila did not last long in power. He soon "fell out" with his Rwandan and Ugandan sponsors when he tried to exercise some independence, to which they did not take too kindly. After a little over one year of rule, in August 1998, Rwanda and Uganda invaded the Congo for the second time. Kabila, facing imminent defeat, called upon his Southern African Development Community (SADC) allies (mainly Zimbabwe, Angola and Namibia) to save the day. This set up a conflict where on one side was Rwanda, Uganda and Burundi and the other side Zimbabwe, Angola and Namibia. The result was the launching of what Madeline Albright would later characterize as Africa's first world war. The war ensnared as many as nine African countries at varying times throughout the conflict. A report by the World Policy Institute noted that the United States has supplied weapons and training to eight of the nine nations involved in the Congo war.[2]

This second Congo war [i.e., invasion by Rwanda and Uganda] would quickly become what the International Rescue Committee say is the deadliest conflict since World War Two. According to *The Lancet* and the International Rescue Committee almost 4 million Congolese died in a six-year period, most of those deaths from preventable and treatable diseases and starvation.[3] Over 77 percent of the deaths took place in five Eastern provinces of the Congo bordering Uganda and Rwanda and affected mainly children. Almost half of the deaths occurred among children five years old and younger.[4]

The war lasted from 1998 to 2003, a period that witnessed myriad corporate and foreign predators descending on the Congo to pick at the carcass of a state. Laurent Desire Kabila was assassinated during this period, on January 16, 2001, one day before the anniversary of Lumumba's assassination on January 17, 1961. His son Joseph Kabila took over the leadership of the Congo and presided over a peace process that led to a transition government and elections. Rwanda and Uganda had to withdraw from the Congo but they both have proxies in the Congo with Rwanda being the prime culprit. The East of the country is still simmering in conflict and according to the International Rescue Committee reports approximately 1,000 Congolese are dying each day.[5]

The list of corporate beneficiaries of the Congo war is staggering.[6] The United Nations published four reports from 2001 to 2003 where it documented the illegal exploitation of the natural resources of the Congo and listed the companies implicated in the pilfering of Congo's resources.[7]

Congo is the quintessential example on the African continent of how conflict is used to benefit a coterie of elites within and outside of the country. Multinational corporations are not averse to establishing relations with rebel leaders while they are in the bush, as American Mineral Fields and Bechtel did with Laurent Kabila in 1997.[8] The United Nations has accused the US-based Cabot Corporation of supporting war crimes, violating human rights, and despoiling the environment in the Congo.[9]

Today, whether one calls it neo-colonialism, neo-liberalism, globalization, or the Washington Consensus, the fundamental structure remains the same, one in which the strong dominates and exploits the weak by whatever means is at their disposal.

Further Reading

De Witte, Ludo. *The Assassination of Lumumba*. Verso, 2001. Translation by Ann Wright and Renee Fenby, 2001.

Hochschild, Adam. *King Leopold's Ghost: A Story of Greed, Terror, and Heroism In Colonial Africa*. First Mariner Books, 1999.

Kalb, Madeleine. *Congo Cables:The Cold War in Africa—From Eisenhower to Kennedy.* MacMillan Publishing, 1982.

Kanza, Thomas. *Rise and Fall of Patrice Lumumba: Conflict in the Congo*. London, England: Rex Collings, Ltd., 1978.

Nkrumah, Kwame. *Challenge of the Congo*. New York: International Publishers, 1967.

Nzongola-Ntalaja, Georges. *The Congo: From Leopold to Kabila: A People's History*. Nordiska Afrikainstitutet, 2005.

Rodney, Walter. *How Europe Underdeveloped Africa*. Howard University Press, 1981.

16

ILLUSION

*The environmental consequences of wars
are insignificant.*

War poses the largest environmental problem
in human history.

Tom Hastings

Hiroshima, Nagasaki, Vietnam, Belgrade, Iraq, Afghanistan — just a few of the places whose ecological devastation by war is well-known. But even France can suffer an increasingly rare instance of white phosphorus landmine injury or death when some farmer or construction worker hits live ordnance planted during the Franco-German War of 1870! One hundred and ten million buried explosive devices still pollute the soils of our planet, chemicals used in military materiel manufacture and routine operations are contaminating groundwater from Massachusetts to Diego Garcia; depleted uranium testing rounds foul the waters of the Mississippi from Minnesota on down; and the crystal clear waters around Aviano in Italy are befouled by USAF hazardous waste that migrates from the hangars to the hydrology.

In general, humanity is overconsuming resources, and the Pentagon is the worst abuser.

In one day the world uses up oil that took 110,000 years to fossilize.... About a quarter of the world's jet fuel is consumed by military aircraft. The gas mileage on an F-16 is so bad that it consumes in 30 minutes what the average motorist does in a year.[1]

War is the largest environmental problem in human history. The Pentagon is the single largest consumer of fossil fuels on Earth and is also the primary instrument of more disastrous pollution due to its fuel use during war. It contributes massively to the global warming process. Domestically, the U.S. Department of Defense (DoD) and its supplying manufacturers are responsible for more Superfund sites, and for more "environmental hotspots" than any other entity. With more than 700 bases on the soil of at least 130 other nation-states, our environmental disregard extends around the world in tandem with our military. This problem is pandemic, worldwide, and worst in the case of the U.S. because the U.S. has such a massive military, and especially an enormous arsenal and transport sector.

As the *Ecologist* pointed out:

- The US Department of Defence (DOD) generates 750,000 tons of hazardous waste per year, more than the five largest chemical companies combined.
- There are 400 metric tons of weapons grade plutonium in the world today, most of it in the US and former Soviet military stockpiles.[2] One millionth of an ounce of inhaled plutonium oxide dust will cause lung cancer in humans.
- As a result of naval accidents, at least 50 nuclear warheads and 11 nuclear reactors litter the ocean floor.[3]

As I've spoken about this across the U.S. over the past 14 years, veterans approach me with stories of fuel dumping, waste dumping and prolific overuse of fuel. They tell me about dumping more than 20,000 gallons of jet fuel from a ship in order to show that they need a full funding allotment for the next period. They tell me of routine airborne fuel dumping from C-130s because the aircraft will snap wings if landing with too much fuel. They tell me of hideously radioactive clandestine "disposal" on the high seas and in port from our nuclear-powered craft, both boats and ships. These men are not proud to be a part of such attacks on the very biosphere, but that is what war is— that, and the training for it.

The Pentagon and its industries protect the American public's right to be informed by keeping all their activities well wrapped in the cloak of "national security." Indeed, it is just that cloak that prevents those so inclined from voluntarily acting responsibly. National security and emissions trading are two peas in a philosophical pod. They both offer rationalizations for bad behavior.[4] Ending both these excuses to pollute would go a long way toward establishing some good faith with those who care about the state of our ecology.

Military pollution affects babies born today—fifty years after the fact. A Peter Eisler story in *USA Today* from 14 October 2004 makes note:

> Amy Ford's baby girl was just learning to crawl last year when men in respirators and hazardous materials suits showed up

at the family's suburban home to tear out the yard. Since then, workers have hauled away tons of asbestos-laced soil from the new development of $500,000 houses. The pollution is a vestige of Lowry Air Force Base, which closed in 1994 and was sold for $8 million to a redevelopment agency set up by the cities of Denver and Aurora. The 1,800-acre site now supports 2,800 homes, schools, shopping areas, offices and parks.[5]

The projected cost of cleaning up just the U.S. military bases on U.S. soil will "dwarf the $300-billion federal Superfund program."[6] And it is due now.

Post-conflict Environmental Assessment: Vietnam

The suffering of Vietnam did not end with the liberation of Saigon in 1975. Perhaps no country since Haiti has come to independence under such adverse conditions—conditions which included environmental damage on a scale hitherto unseen in warfare. The damage was not the accidental by-product of war, but part of the attrition strategy which deliberately aimed to drive the peasants into the cities in order to deprive the National Liberation Front of a population and food base, and safe jungle havens.[7]

Concern about the environmental impact of war prior to the Vietnam War was quite rare.[8] Prodded in part by the public interest scientific assessments of the environmental consequences of the war in Vietnam urged by Margaret Mead and conducted by Arthur H. Westing, a relatively thorough analysis of the environmental effects of the war in that poor country revealed massive damage to soil, water and forest cover. The chemical contamination introduced by dioxin-laden Agent Orange and its other chemical defoliants added to the bomb cratering and general military pollution achieved, in part, what Air Force general Curtis LeMay had threatened—to "bomb them back into the Stone Age." Sadly for Vietnam, the Stone Age at least was pristine while the post-U.S.-war environment was toxic. One wonders if the Agent Orange victims might have happily chosen the Stone Age without modern benefits—if it came without the military pollution that has so disfigured and disabled them.

Pentagon Waste Greater Danger than Terrorist Attack

Every year Project Censored, based at Sonoma State University in California, issues its top 25 stories that should have been big but weren't. In 2006, the 15th story was a compilation of reports on the Pentagon's pollution of the U.S. From their report:

> The world's largest polluter, the U.S. military, generates 750,000
> tons of toxic waste material annually, more than the five largest
> chemical companies in the U.S. combined. This pollution
> occurs globally as the U.S. maintains bases in dozens of
> countries. Not only is the military emitting toxic material directly
> into the air and water, it's poisoning the land of nearby
> communities resulting in increased rates of cancer, kidney
> disease, increasing birth defects, low birth weight, and
> miscarriage.[9]

A *USA Today* map shows 130 environmental catastrophes
produced in 39 states by our own military "protecting" our land.[10] With
defenders like these, who needs outside assault? Imagine if China had
infiltrated the port at Bangor, Washington and polluted it so badly with
chemical sediments that the US Environmental Protection Agency declared
it a Superfund site in 1990 as a result. What would we want to do to China?

More insidious than the general pollution generated by the
military is the racial bias its half-baked attempt at disposal demonstrates.
"In Memphis, Tennessee, a military depot dumped chemical weapons in
the midst of a black residential community without informing people of the
health dangers. Today, women there report a high incidence of miscarriage,
birth defects, kidney diseases, and cancer."[11] This has been true at Native
American reservations and communities of color across the U.S. and is
part of the reason the Civil Rights Act of 1964 was a part of environmental
justice as it was written into federal environmental law during the Clinton
administration.

Off the contiguous 48 states, the situation hardly gets better; if
anything, it worsens. While the name Naval Computer and Telecommunications Area Master Station Eastern Pacific hardly conjures up notions of
serious contamination, this DoD facility at Wahlawa, Hawaii, on Oahu,
was declared a Superfund site in 1994 for its disastrous soil contamination.
What if Basher al-Asad had been caught leading a team of polluters and
they had done this to "our" Hawaii? And what of Vieques?

Conclusions and Solutions

There are alternatives to the military. Peace scholars of many
stripes have shown this for many years. Using nonviolence to manage our
conflicts, as it has been employed in liberation struggles from Gandhi's
India to Ukraine, would result in fewer environmental problems.

A 2005 Freedom House study examined 67 regime changes in the last 33 years and found the metrics of sustainable democracy, enduring human rights and civil rights were statistically substantially higher when mass liberatory nonviolence was used to bring down dictators:[12]

> In November-December 2004, the international community was surprised by the scale and perseverance of nonviolent civic resistance in Ukraine, as millions of citizens successfully pressed for free and fair elections in what became known as the Orange Revolution. But Ukraine's Orange Revolution was only the latest in a series of successful "people power" revolutions that include the Philippines in 1986; Chile and Poland, in 1988; Hungary, East Germany, and Czechoslovakia in 1989; the Baltic States in 1991; South Africa in 1994; Serbia and Peru in 2000; and Georgia in 2003.

We have choices. We need to hear from the experts who don't have a stake in the status quo, who have ethics, and who might like history to recall them fondly. The environmental professionals who act as though patriotism means only focusing on non-military pollution are not up to the task. It is painfully clear that passing laws is never going to be enough when the outbreak of war sets aside concern for the environment under the exigencies of bloody conflict.[13] The only cure for war's impact on the Earth is to prepare for peace instead of war — prepare, that is, to pursue our objectives by any nonviolent means at our command.

Further Reading

Bannon, Ian and Collier, Paul. *Natural Resources and Violent Conflict: Options and Actions*. Washington DC: The World Bank, 2003.

Klare, Michael T., *Blood and Oil: The Dangers and Consequences of America?s Growing Petroleum Dependency*. New York: Henry Holt and Company, 2004.

Klare, Michael T., *Resource Wars The New Landscape of Global Conflict*. New York: Metropolitan Books, 2001.

Worldwatch Institute, *State of the World 2005*. New York: W.W. Norton & Company Ltd., 2005.

Paul W. Tibbets, Jr., pilot of the nuclear attack on Hiroshima, is enshrined with honor into the National Aviation Hall of Fame. The attack is claimed to have brought about a quicker surrender from the enemy and a reduction in the loss of Allied lives, but this notion has been widely challenged. (See http://www.doug-long.com/quotes.htm for a list of citations from prominent Americans, including Dwight D. Eisenhower and Albert Einstein, challenging both the need and the morality of the use of nuclear weapons on civilian populations.) The bombs killed as many as 140,000 people in Hiroshima by the end of 1945. Since then, thousands more have died from injuries or illness attributed to exposure to radiation. A number of notable individuals and organizations have criticized the bombings, many of them characterizing them as war crimes or crimes against humanity. Today the US is engaged in the further development of "tactical" nuclear weapons, and through Presidential Decision Directive PPD 60, has reserved the right to use nuclear weapons against non-nuclear states.

REALISM

War is inevitable

Is war someday to become obsolete because of ever more frightening weapons? An English editor wrote about the gun in 1715: *But perhaps Heaven hath in Judgment inflicted the Cruelty of this Invention, on purpose to fright Men into Amity and Peace, and into an Abhorrence of the Tumult and Inhumanity of War.*[1] In a similar way Alfred Nobel hoped that his invention of dynamite would eradicate war.[2] Just a few years before World War 1 Englishman Norman Angell wrote "Europe's Optical Illusion," which argued that economic integration throughout Europe had made war ineffective and obsolete.[3] The development of the atomic bomb re-ignited this thinking, although less than a month after the testing of the first working atomic weapon at Los Alamos, the United States used it to end World War 2.

Is war inevitable because of the natural malevolence and aggressiveness of humans? Conservative Christians might say yes, based on sentiments like those of John Calvin, who spoke of human natures 'abominable to God' and subject to punishment but for the grace of our savior. Muslims are instructed by the Qur'an that, while they do not like fighting, it is still incumbent upon them, but only if it is a war of self-defense or against oppression. In the Hindu Bhagavad Gita, the hero is urged to kill if duty so demands, and the 'karma yoga' of battle is praised as a high ideal. Great thinkers like Immanuel Kant, Baruch Spinoza, Martin Luther, and John Milton generally concurred.[4] Sigmund Freud and Albert Einstein agreed in their correspondence to each other that "man has within him a lust for hatred and destruction." William James felt that war is innate and emotionally appealing.

In 1986, on the other hand, a group of scientists and scholars affiliated with the United Nations Educational, Scientific and Cultural Organization (UNESCO) issued the Seville Statement on Violence, which asserts the scientific incorrectness of believing that mankind is naturally warlike. Anthropologist Douglas Fry compiled a list of 74 cultures around the world who were 'nonwarring,' based on a definition of war as a group activity involving one community against another, in which the primary purpose is to inflict serious injury or death on members of the other side.[5] He also identified countries that rarely go to war, such as Sweden, Switzerland, and Iceland.

Comprehensive studies from other researchers came to the same conclusion: societies exist who do not make war.[6] A classic WW2-era study by Quincy Wright categorized 590 world societies by their affinity for warfare.[7] Nearly 2/3 of this sizable sample were considered either nonwarring (5%) or mild-warring (59%).

We may never know the truth about humankind's propensity for war. But from a purely practical viewpoint, it seems likely to continue. Those placed above us counsel us to accept what we cannot change, rather than attempt to change what we don't understand. Compliance on our part can save a lot of time and energy. Those viewed as 'realistic' seem to be endowed with a clear-headedness that implies productiveness.

Is the military solution, in the long run, the reality we must learn to accept, or are there alternatives? For the sake of our children and their future well-being, we must make a better effort to answer this question.

17

ILLUSION

I personally have no better options
than joining the military.

REALITY

**There are numerous non-military means by which
to find a job, obtain an education, or enhance life chances.**

Amy Meyers

> "The military is not a social welfare agency;
> it's not a jobs program...
> The goal of the military is to fight and win wars."
> — **Dick Cheney, then Secretary of Defense**

Do you see military recruiters more often than you see college or job recruiters? Is the military the only agency that seems to be offering you viable options to a successful future? The military uses money for college, job training, and bonuses as incentives to get you to enlist, but not because it is genuinely concerned about your civilian education or job. You do have other options!

Most people join the military with the goal to get ahead - build character, learn practical job skills, and/or get a college education. Military advertising centers on these ideals. Oftentimes, enlistees are under the misconception that military service will solve their problems and provide them with more attractive opportunities for the future. The military becomes an especially attractive option when other opportunities seem scarce. However, many end up disappointed when they don't get the skills and benefits they were promised or had hoped for.

Militarization Through Education

The military is infiltrating America's educational institutions. This is evident with the high profile military academies and programs; Reserve Officer Training Corps (ROTC)—College level, Junior Reserve Officer

Training Corps (JROTC)—High school level and Cadet Corps—middle school level. Although the Department of Defense (DOD) claims these programs are not recruiting tools, they are a mechanism for enforcing *military indoctrination*, and they are growing at an alarming rate. Many believe these programs are designed to instill discipline, which they may do—but they also teach mindless obedience which limits the capacity to be self-directed. Most military programs and/or academies are located within schools of working class communities with populations predominated by minorities. In many circumstances, it's much easier to talk to a military recruiter than to a college advisor or an employment recruiter. Even in the absence of a military program on campus, the 'No Child Left Behind' Act provides recruiters the right to obtain students' personal contact information, as well as the space and opportunity to approach students within the schools. The School Recruiting Program isn't widely discussed in our communities, but the US Army Recruiting Command Training SRP (School Recruiting Program) Handbook explicitly states the program is:

· Designed to assist recruiters in penetrating their school market and channeling their efforts through specific tasks and goals to obtain the maximum number of quality recruits.[1]
· Critical to both short term and long-term recruiting success. Remember, first to contact, first to contract.[2]

Only 10% of recruits initiate the recruitment process themselves. Family and friends (known to the military as 'influencers') increasingly discourage enlistment. In response, the military employs systematic, inventive methods to attract students using methods that parents may be unaware of. The military spent $3.9 billion on a wide variety of recruitment activities in 2006.[3]

The military, particularly the Army, often evokes strong positive 'values' like loyalty, duty, integrity and courage.[4] These values are clearly admirable, but can be instilled without military influence. School administrators, teachers, coaches, counselors, parents and community members should promote these values by providing environments conducive to fostering them; and by focusing on academic achievement, positive social development and self reliance. It is not the business or responsibility of the military to build character in our youth. We must demand that our schools focus on these positive qualities. We cannot remain complacent, accepting our schools' shortcomings and relying on military programs to set things right. Schools are meant for educating, not for the military to do their bidding.

Military propaganda

Since World War I, the military's presence in our lives has steadily increased, and has been accepted with little opposition. Americans have become conditioned to the message of the military, using enlistment as a path for reaching goals, achieving discipline, learning new skills, and serving your country. Little emphasis is placed on the actual goal of the military – to fight and win wars!

Similar to large corporations, the military seeks to increase and improve its standing in public perception, and to enhance its popularity amongst its citizens. Billions of dollars are spent each year on various recruiting and marketing tactics: colorful advertisements, brochures, commercials, video games, personal visits, hundreds of hyped-up military career choices, money for college and possible bonuses. Through the military's public relations campaign and cultural subversion, people lose sight of the goals and true purpose of the military.

Boston Globe

The U.S. Army sponsors the NASCAR NEXTEL Cup and racing teams. Nielsen Sports™ rated the Army the winning sponsor of the 2007 NASCAR Cup Daytona 500. According to the *Boston Globe*, NASCAR is the Army's top program for generating leads for its recruiters.

"Good advertising does not just circulate information. It penetrates the public mind with desires and belief," according to the ad agency Leo Burnett. By the end of 1990s recruitment was down and 'Be

All You Can Be' was no longer working. "Kids don't like it" said Ray DeThorne of Leo Burnett, which took over PR for the Army and produced 'The Army of One' campaign[5]; "It's a clever campaign, but substantially dishonest. The Army is not, never has been, and never will be about one soldier. Individuality has absolutely nothing to do with Army life" said Bob Garfield, ad critic for Advertising Age.[6]

According to a government case study, it was recommended that the military build a values-based ad campaign highlighting the advantages of joining the military, emphasizing that military service helps develop character and discipline. The military should encourage and highlight the option of the military as a career, providing valuable skills and education opportunities. Strategically, the communications need to augment the pride that comes from having a successful child with the pride unique to serving one's country.[7] The revised DOD advertising campaign, built on Harris Interactive's values-based recommendations above, is currently running under the 'Army of One' theme directly addressing youth enlistment and parents' proud support. Meanwhile the Army National Guard has shifted from costly television ads to appeals that are more narrowly targeted at the young, such as pitches on pizza boxes and iTunes giveaways.[8]

Truths of a Militarized Society

Militarization has been ingrained in us over the years, and the result is a type of complacency towards an ever more *militarized society*. Various high-tech, high-budget military marketing campaigns including television commercials and print and radio advertisements have become the norm. Opportunities for young adults include going to college, finding a decent job, or joining the military. But in actuality some sectors of American youth are steered in the direction of military enlistment far more aggressively than toward the other options, and may not be aware that viable alternatives can and do exist for them. Society as a whole needs to stop accepting ideas pushed on them through fancy marketing campaigns and discouraging social/economic circumstances, and act to change the status quo. Accepting the military as a tool to uplift our youth and point them in the right direction is like condoning violence as a way to advance in life. The military is a place for responsible adults, not a place for youth still developing their concept of accountability.

Again, the goal of the military is to fight and win wars, oftentimes provoking the 'enemy' with aggression. The military has become a machine whose primary purpose is no longer focused on defense but on power and profit, using its members as expendable toys, while countless pay a profound price and few profit. Major General Smedley Butler made it clear in 1935 that 'war is a racket' and it remains true today.[9]

The military boasts of promoting ethical behavior and, as noted above, upholding values associated with serving. Army ethics rest at the bedrock of the seven Army values: Loyalty, Duty, Respect, Selfless Service, Honor, Integrity and Personal Courage...a unique collection, unlike any other organization in the world, and reflecting the high standards to which the *entire* Army adheres, regardless of its mission area.[10]

It would be hard to find anyone that does not admire such values. However, these values are not easily measurable, and oftentimes contradictory to situations service members face when challenged by personal moral values. Meanwhile, the military provides little substance behind the words themselves, by actually training and ensuring such values are met and held by *all* service members. For example, some current issues that have plagued the Iraq War provide proof of the contradictions and degradation of the values that all supposedly adhere to: Blackwater USA, private security contractors who are mainly veterans of the US Military, have been consistently accused of overstepping boundaries and committing homicide; the US Marine civilian slaughter in Haditha amongst other similar cases; and the US Military operated prison detainee torture/abuse scandal at Abu Ghraib. Obviously there is a lapse in the bedrock of the military's highly esteemed ethical values when such atrocities exist, and consequences for those that do not adhere to these values are nearly nonexistent.

Militarism permeates society, underhandedly promoting war by using fear, patriotism, democracy and freedom to get the public to buy into it. By refocusing some of the DOD's colossal budget on greatly needed social programs, improved quality of life and work towards peace could be afforded. The United States spends almost a trillion dollars a year on war-related expenses, while almost nothing is invested in peaceful interaction with the rest of the world. Even today, contradictions of the military's integrity, war's aggression and the dire need for improved social programs at home continue to be far too prevalent.

> America would never invest the necessary funds or energies in rehabilitation of its poor so long as adventures like Vietnam continued to draw men and skills and money like some demonic, destructive suction tube. So I increasingly compelled to see the war as an enemy of the poor...the war is doing far more than devastating the hopes of the poor at home...I could never again raise my voice against the violence of the oppressed in the ghettos without having first spoken clearly to the greatest purveyor of violence in the world today: my own government...It should be incandescently clear that no one who has any concern for the integrity and life of America today can ignore the present war...A nation that continues

year after year to spend more money on military defense than on programs of social uplift is approaching spiritual death.
— Dr. Martin Luther King, Jr.[11]

The military does not promote nonviolent resolutions or equality; it consists of and enforces violence, competition and hierarchical relationships. The system itself fosters violence and discrimination. The military places numerous restrictions on personal behavior, and service members are taught to obey and not question orders and are subject to military law 24 hours a day, even when off duty or off base. Quitting the military for whatever reason is not an option. Disobedience, absence without leave, etc. can lead to criminal punishment, court martial, prison and/or dishonorable discharge — all of which negate military promises and impact a soldier's future in the civilian world.

Military recruiters are sales people presenting one positive side of a very complex issue. Many recruiters are under great pressure to succeed in enlisting new recruits, which can lead to misrepresentation of benefits or withholding unpleasant truths. Some promise jobs and training, when in fact they have no power to fulfill such promises. Many fail to mention the serious problems that plague military life. Despite assumptions; the military does not protect you from discrimination, racism, sexism, homophobia or gang problems.

Minorities make up over 30% of the enlisted military, but only 12% of the officers. They are more likely to be given low-level jobs, to be passed up for promotion, and to end up on the front lines of combat. Discrimination against gays, lesbians and bisexuals is official military procedure with the "Don't Ask, Don't Tell" policy. Women are still limited in the positions open to them and are often given traditional administrative tasks; one in three females report being victims to rape or attempted rape, while three out of four experience sexual harassment. Equal opportunity within the military is not practiced policy.

People have the right to base important life decisions on clear and accurate information, not myths, stretched truths, or overextended promises. These DOD programs and marketing schemes rob our schools and communities of money, and they deflect students from pursuing workable alternatives for education or employment by providing false promises of military life and insinuating violence and war as heroic, patriotic and admirable. Sadly, there are no comparable advocacy agencies or budgets for the promotion of peace and community improvement.

The Truth about Military Job Training/Skills

The enlistment contract for the Army (other service branches contain similar language) states 'If the Secretary of the Army determines for reasons of military necessity or national security members are available for immediate reassignment, any guarantees…may be terminated. Under these conditions I may be reassigned according to the needs of the Army.' This can easily result in a change to significantly more risky, less desirable duty. The enlistment agreement also has a clause expressing that a recruit's pay, benefits and responsibilities in the military can change without warning regardless of any promises made in the agreement.

Why are terms and conditions of the enlistment contract entitled to change without your consent or notice? Why aren't you allowed to change your mind or quit without facing serious repercussions?

Military training is designed for military jobs, not for subsequent civilian jobs. Most jobs are assigned to recruits based on the military's need to fill that specific job. And most require specific skills that don't translate from the military to the civilian market. Training and experience don't always coincide either. Even if you get the training promised for a particular occupation you may not receive on-the-job experience. Furthermore, many jobs with impressive titles are actually low-skilled or non-technical positions.

Mangum and Ball, Ohio State Researchers who received funding from the military, found that only 12% of male veterans and 6% of female veterans surveyed made any use of skills learned in the military in their civilian jobs.[12] Stephen Barley, a labor policy specialist, found that the average recent veteran will earn between 11% and 19% less than non-veterans from comparable socio-economic backgrounds.[13] The job of your choice outside of the military is not guaranteed after your service terminates. The military won't make you financially secure. Military members are no strangers to financial strain: 48% report having financial difficulty, approximately 33% of homeless men in the United States are veterans, and nearly 200,000 veterans are homeless on any given night.[14]

The Real Scoop on Money from the Military for College

Over the years individuals have stated that money for college was one of the dominant reasons for enlisting in the Army.[15] Many people are attracted by the promises of tens of thousands of dollars for college. The reasoning for offering such benefits is 'to encourage college-capable individuals to defer their college until they have served.'[16] This is not free money! You sign a contract for 8 years and during that period you are working for the military, oftentimes with your education on hold. The money is not guaranteed upon discharge, for only if you meet all of the requirements can you collect. But even then, the amount is usually less than the promised amount. Initially, you have to invest $1200 of your own money within your first year, and this is non-refundable. If you receive a less-than-honorable discharge (as 1 in 4 do), leave the military early (as 1 in 3 do), or do not attend college, you do not recoup any of that money, not even your $1200 deposit. Only about half of eligible veterans use their educational benefits. According to the US Veterans Administration, only 35% of veterans receive Montgomery GI Bill (MGIB) funds for college, which means 65% of recruits who pay the mandatory $1200 into the MGIB never see that money in return.[17]

Getting the GI Bill does not mean all of your college will be paid for and it is not easy to collect. Marine Corps Veteran Matt Howard shares his experience:

> They told me I would get all this money for college... I was so naïve that I didn't know it wasn't enough to cover school, they were very convincing... I was so disgusted by how hard it was to get my college benefits, I just gave up... I volunteered for the Marines, served in Iraq...the military sells itself on money for college; it is the major recruitment tool. This is supposedly why I sold my soul to the devil.[18]

Even the Department of Defense admits that educational benefits are typically the major recruiting inducement. Yet only 15% of enlistees actually go on to graduate with a four-year college/university degree.

Finding a Non-military Job

Finding a job that offers decent pay, benefits, and personal enjoyment is not an easy task, but it is possible with sufficient preparation. Apprenticeships are paid work agreements that lead to certification in various fields/skills/trades (examples: electrician, mechanic, barber...). Internships, paid and unpaid positions, provide training and experience in certain fields. American Friends Service Committee's *Great Careers* booklet provides an overview of alternatives to the military.[19] Some of the recommendations stand out as particularly appealing with today's growing service industries: computer technology, culinary arts, auto mechanics, medicine and health. An aging population ensures a steady need for health practitioners. A fundamental knowledge of word processing and spreadsheet development can lead to an entry level job or provide enhancement in an existing clerical position.

There are many other occupations that offer the opportunity to grow, while helping your community and influencing social change: artists, teachers, medics, organizers, social workers, environmentalists, lobbyists, journalists, etc. These types of positions are usually offered by more specific issue-targeted organizations.[20] Listed below are some resources to check out:

· America's Job Bank (guides to finding a job). <www.ajb.org>.

· Job Corps (job training and support from US Department of Labor for low income youth). <www.jobcorps.doleta.gov>;
· Employment & Training / US Dept of Labor. <www.doleta.gov>;

· Inroads Home (leadership training and internships for minority youth). <www.inroads.org>;

· Idealist Social Action (jobs and volunteer opportunities that include education and travel). <www.idealist.org>;

· Social Service job opportunities. <www.socialservice.com>, <www.appleseednetwork.org>;

· Americorps, VISTA (Combines jobs, travel, community service and training with ways to earn money for college and relief from student loans). <www.americorps.org>, <www.nationalservices.org>.

Update your resume and outline all of your skills. Include any work or volunteer experiences you may have—even those activities which you might have done only for fun, such as organizing a sports event or other group activity. Take time to figure out short and long term goals, and the types of jobs that interest you. Seek input from people who have positions that may be suitable. Update your references (these should be reliable non-family member contacts you've known for more than one year) and notify them that you are listing them as employment references. Your appearance at an interview is equally important. Dress the part; be prepared, courteous and confident.

Non-military Means for Funding College

Financing college is expensive and complicated, but there are solutions to subsidizing the expense of college. School costs vary, as well as the amount of available financial aid. Finding scholarships and other forms of aid can be a time-consuming and boring task. Searching and applying for financial aid, scholarships, and grants is well worth your time though. Seventy percent of students who apply for financial aid end up qualifying and receiving funds.

Financial aid is based on the level of financial need. To determine this, you must complete the Free Application for Federal Student Aid (FAFSA).[21] Federal Aid is calculated by the cost of the school you plan to attend minus your family's expected contribution (which is determined through FAFSA). The form is long and confusing, so don't be afraid to ask for help in completing it. Make sure to complete and send it according to deadlines. Within 4-6 weeks you will receive your Student Aid Report (SAR)[22] showing your family's expected contribution and the amount of federal aid for which you are eligible, including loans (borrowed money, you pay back), grants (free money, you do not pay back) and on-campus work-study programs. Having this information will start you on your quest to find more monies at your chosen college, which may have additional financial aid, scholarships, and grants available.

Although scholarships are mainly awarded for academic or athletic superiority, there are many scholarships available for people with specific skills, interests, majors, and for specific ethnic and/or religious backgrounds. There are numerous websites that offer free tools in scholarship searches.[23] Finding the funding to go to college is challenging, but the payoff can be great!

Attending a 2-year junior/community college will save money. Tuition and fees are usually much less that at the 4-year universities. They are a particularly good choice for completing your required general education courses. Earning an associate's degree and then transferring to a university can save you tens of thousands of dollars.

Think before you enlist

With the end of conscription, the military has relied heavily on limited economic opportunities to compel youth into enlisting, also known as the *poverty draft*. As college costs continue to rise, cost of living increases and employment wages do not keep up; the big promises made by the military become more enticing for many. You should not enlist simply because other options seem scarce or harder to obtain.

Serious moral questions should be considered prior to signing any contract with the military. Conscientious Objection[24] is hard to obtain, especially in the 'volunteer military.' Ask yourself: Can you kill men, women or children? Can you kill for ideologies that you do not understand or agree with? Are you willing to risk your safety, health, life, moral obligations, and mentality for something you are unable to control or may not understand? If you answered no to any of these questions, you need to do more personal exploration. Resources for more information on this are located at the end of the chapter, and are easily obtainable in various books and websites.

Due to the American 'war-on-terror,' and ongoing bloody wars in Afghanistan and Iraq, the military is having increasing difficulty convincing young people to enlist and getting parents to support enlistment. So recruiters will be trying even harder to get you now. A new ploy uses current guard members to do the recruiting by targeting their friends and neighborhood contacts. The Army National Guard in New Hampshire and 21 other states is offering a $2,000 bonus to Guard members who get a buddy to sign up…the latest sign that dangerous wartime deployments make this a challenging time for military recruiters. Some veterans' groups fear the monetary incentive will be a disincentive to tell the truth about risks.[25] Don't be fooled—The Army National Guard and Army Reserves purpose is not confined to domestic issues; they can and do serve in war. They've supplied approximately forty percent of the troops in the Iraq war, started in 2003.

Don't buy into all of the propaganda provided by Uncle Sam. Is joining the military something that *you* have wanted for a long time, or a hasty decision you may regret later? Don't make this decision when you are upset, confused, feeling lost, pressured or unsure. If you think the military is the right path for you, make sure to read the enlistment contract carefully. You can take the contract home to study it and have others look it over with you. Know that once you reach basic training you are required to fulfill the entire contract (usually eight total years, four active and four as Inactive Ready Reserve). You have no control over the military changing your contract terms (pay, job, benefits). Your constitutional rights are severely restricted; you are required to follow orders given to you, whether you consider them fair or not, moral or not. You cannot leave on your own terms. You cannot quit or demand a discharge, but the military can discharge you without your consent. Remember the contract favors the military—not you!

Getting Out: What You Should Know

The *Delayed Entry Program* (DEP)[26], sometimes referred as the Delayed Enlistment Program, allows recruiters to more efficiently make assignments by giving recruits a specific date for reporting for active duty, up to 365 days. Not incidentally, it facilitates recruitment by easing enlistees into the process. Recruiters work on quotas, like a sales person, and while many are genuine and sincere, some are not always forthright. Remember that the recruiter's job is to get individuals to enlist; they are not your friend!

Getting out of the DEP is indeed possible. Regulations governing the Army, Navy, Marines, Air Force and Coast Guard (every branch of service) are the same with the DEP. The DEP is a legal, binding contract. However it is official policy of the DOD that anyone can request to be released from the Delayed Enlistment Program. Department of Defense Directive 1332.14, Enlisted Administrative Separations, and individual service recruiting regulations allow anyone in the DEP to request a separation from the Delayed Enlistment Program. Most DEP discharge requests are approved. Even in those few cases where a recruiting commander disapproves the request, if the applicant refuses to ship out to basic training, absolutely nothing happens to them. If a recruiter or anyone else tells you that you can't get out of the DEP, they are lying to you. A DEP discharge is officially known as an 'Entry Level Separation' (ELS). An ELS is not characterized as Honorable, General, or Other Than Honorable. A DEP Discharge does not result in an RE (Reenlistment Eligibility) Code that will prevent joining the same or another military service in the future.[27] Most importantly, it should be understood that the DEP does not qualify you for active duty and you do not have to obey any military orders.

There are numerous non-military means by which to find a job or obtain an education. There are economic and educational alternatives to military enlistment; reaching these may not be as easy as signing an enlistment contract, but they are there and should be seriously considered! Joining the military is not something you should do because other options seem scarce. Think about it and talk to veterans before you sign over the next 8 years of your life.

> "By blindly honoring the uniform and glorifying the military, we will fail to prevent the next war...We must get active in the community...we must stop the military from creeping into our schools, our communities, and our homes."[28]
>
> —Evan Knappenberger, IVAW

Further Reading

Allison, Aimee and Solnit, David. *Army of None: Strategies to Counter Military Recruitement, End War, and Build a Better World.* Seven Stories Press, 2007

Bacevich, Andrew J. *The New American Militarism.* Oxford University Press, 2005.

Cortright, David. *Soldiers in Revolt.* Haymarket Press, 2006.

Crawford, John. *The Last True Story I'll Ever Tell.* Riverhead Trade, 2006.

Ehrhart, Jan and W.D. *Demilitarized Zones: Veterans After Vietnam.* East River Anthology, 1976.

American Wars: Illusions and Realities / edited by Paul Buchheit

Ketwig, John. A*nd a Hard Rain Fell: A GI's True Story of War in Vietnam*. Longman Pub Group, 2004.

Zinn, Howard. P*eople's History of the United States*. Harper Perennial Modern Classics, 2005.

Heller, Joseph. *Catch 22*

Butler, Smedley Major General. *War Is a Racket*, 1935.

Recommended Websites

Counter Recruitment, <http://www.counter-recruitment.org>
GI Rights Hotline, <http://www.girights.org>
Vietnam Veterans Against the War, <http:// www.vvaw.org>
Veterans for Peace, <http://www.vfp.org>
Iraq Veterans Against the War, <http://www.ivaw.org>
The Project on Youth and Nonmilitary Opportunities (Project YANO), <http://www.projectyano.org>

Recommended Films

When I Came Home (based on a homeless Iraq War Veteran)
Sir, No Sir (based on active duty and veterans against the Vietnam War, during the war)
Winter Soldier (based on veterans accounts of Vietnam War and atrocities committed)
Soldiers Speak Out (based on Iraq/Afghanistan War Veterans)
The Ground Truth (based on Iraq/Afghanistan War Veterans)
Chicago Occupied, IVAW First Casualty (based on Iraq/Afghanistan Veterans re-enactment of occupation)

ILLUSION

Wars result from the aggressive nature of human beings.

REALITY

**Anger is natural to human beings, not aggression.
There are non-violent ways to deal with anger.**

Arun Gandhi

Over the centuries, as human beings have traversed the long road to more civilized behavior, they have progressed in every sense except one—their approval of the culture of violence. Since the day a humanoid picked up a club in a fit of anger to bash the head of a perceived enemy, humankind has progressed only to the extent that we now have sophisticated weapons that permit us to wreak mass destruction. Our solutions to disputes remain, for the most part, the same: to overpower our adversaries. In fact, we have so ignored the need to control our violent propensities that we have come to believe that a propensity to violence is just a part of human nature, just as killing is in the nature of predators in the animal kingdom.

But is violence a normal human behavior? If violence, indeed, were innate in human nature, we would not need martial arts institutes and military academies to teach people how to fight and kill. We wouldn't need psychologists and psychiatrists to conduct research on how to mentally tune soldiers to dehumanize the opponent and kill the enemy — or deal with those who suffer afterwards for having done so. Killing would be as natural to us as tearing at the throat of its victim is natural to a lion.

My grandfather, Mohandas K. Gandhi, the father of modern nonviolence, witnessed the unnatural brutality of the supposedly civilized British soldiers during the Zulu Rebellion in 1906 in South Africa. I say "supposedly" because it was the white man who went to Africa and Asia to "civilize" the native heathens. However, as my grandfather describes it, the Zulu Rebellion was no war between equals. The British soldiers were literally hunting down the Zulus like animals and shooting them in the back. It was a brutal massacre. It was this experience that awakened in him a resentment of the culture of violence that brutalizes human societies everywhere.

Is this natural to humanity, and should we just accept this as an unfortunate fact of life? Gandhi refused to believe this, and so he turned this brutal experience into a motivating factor for change. Thus the modern version of the Philosophy of Nonviolence or Culture of Nonviolence was born. Gandhi demonstrated its efficacy in South Africa and in India, and subsequently many others used nonviolence effectively in their own countries—the Soviet Union, Czechoslovakia, Poland, to name a few—and were awarded the Nobel Peace Prize. Instead of working on the concept of nonviolent solutions to conflict and improving upon it, humankind has, for the most part, dismissed the philosophy as an aberration. The consequence is that we have not really understood what Gandhi meant by nonviolence.

The misunderstanding of his philosophy arose because he used it in South Africa and India to win freedom from oppressors, and all attention focused on that alone. Once the objective—liberation—was achieved, we threw the philosophy aside, much as we would a weapon used in combat. It is this attitude, and ignorance, that has given rise to the fallacy that nonviolence is just a strategy to be employed when the conditions are appropriate. But Gandhi said nonviolence is not like a coat that you can wear today and discard tomorrow. Nonviolence must become a part of one's being and eventually replace the culture of violence that dominates every aspect of our lives.

Our relationships, our thoughts, our reactions, our attitudes, our speech, and indeed everything that we do is conditioned by the culture of violence in which we are immersed and from which we have not yet succeeded in emerging. Thus, when we face a conflict with others, our immediate response is violence. This comes so naturally to us that we have come to believe that human beings are inherently violent.

By glorifying violent acts or their perpetrators in history, and depicting violence in movies and media as evidence of bravery, we are insidiously brainwashed into accepting the capacity to inflict violence as a laudable ability. To facilitate our ability to fight and kill, our leaders have devised ways to dehumanize their opponents and then to psychologically induce the rest of us to believe that it is right to kill, that our enemies are inhuman and that they must be eliminated. It was this mindset that made Gandhi ponder what the British were doing to the Zulus in South Africa. I am sure he wondered who the savages in this war were—the so-called uneducated, illiterate black Zulus or the educated British soldiers bearing the white man's burden of civilization.

Gandhi came to the conclusion that what was natural for human beings is not violence but the feeling of anger. He used the analogy of electricity to describe anger in human beings—it is powerful and useful if used intelligently but just as deadly and destructive if abused. Since no one really wants to talk about anger we pay very little attention to this powerful emotion and the result is that most of us abuse anger instead of using that "energy" for positive action. Gandhi said anger is like the trip switch in the electric circuit that warns us of a fault in the distribution line. When responding to this break in the electrical circuit we do so cautiously and intelligently but when responding to anger we lose control and say or do things that often change our lives completely. If we could learn to respond to crises intelligently, we could resolve many problems without bloodshed and remorse. Instead, our egos often override reason, and we conclude that someone who does something we don't like is "bad" or "evil" and must be eliminated.

In the crisis of war that we currently face, did any of us from the President to the media to the people ever ask what motivated the "terrorists" to do what they did on 9/11, or even before that when they attacked us in Kenya and elsewhere? Why are the people in that part of the world so determined to hurt us? To believe and to reflexively state, as the politicians and the media do, that these people are "crazy" and "evil" and must be eliminated at all cost is taking the easy way out. By seeking to understand their hatred and deal with it in a nonviolent way, as Gandhi did, we may find solutions that in the past were obscured by our own aggressive behavior.

Further Reading

Andrews, Charles F. *Mahatma Gandhi—His Life and Ideas*. Radha Publications, 1995.

Dalton, Dennis. *Mahatma Gandhi— Nonviolent Power in Action*. Columbia Univ Press, 1993.

Nanda, B. R. *Mahatma Gandhi—A Biography*. Oxford University Press, 1996.

Rosenberg, Marshall B. *Nonviolent Communication—A Language of Life*. Puddledancer Press, 2003.

ILLUSION

Humans are inevitably driven to war.

REALITY

Blind obedience makes war possible.
Once people know what war is really like, they reject it.

Howard Zinn*

One certain effect of war is to diminish freedom of expression. Patriotism becomes the order of the day, and those who question the war are seen as traitors, to be silenced and imprisoned.

Mark Twain, observing the United States at the turn of the century, its wars in Cuba and the Philippines, described in "The Mysterious Stranger" the process by which wars that are at first seen as unnecessary by the mass of the people become converted into "just" wars:

> The loud little handful will shout for war. The pulpit will warily and cautiously protest at first.... The great mass of the nation will rub its sleepy eyes, and will try to make out why there should be a war, and they will say earnestly and indignantly: "It is unjust and dishonorable and there is no need for war." Then the few will shout even louder.... Before long you will see a curious thing: anti-war speakers will be stoned from the platform, and free speech will be strangled by hordes of furious men who still agree with the speakers but dare not admit it...Next, the statesmen will invent cheap lies, and each man will be glad of these lies, and will study them because they soothe his conscience; and thus he will bye and bye convince himself that the war is just, and he will thank God for a better sleep he enjoys by his self-deception.

*Howard Zinn, "On War" from *The Zinn Reader: Writings on Disobedience and Democracy*. Copyright 1997 by Howard Zinn. Reprinted with the permission of the author and Seven Stories Press, www.sevenstories.com.

My own first impressions of something called war had come at the age of ten, when I read with excitement a series of books about "the boy allies"—A French boy, an English boy, an American boy, and a Russian boy, who became friends, united in the wonderful cause to defeat Germany in World War I. It was an adventure, a romance, told in a group of stories about comradeship and heroism. It was war cleansed of death and suffering.

If anything was left of that romantic view of war, it was totally extinguished when, at eighteen, I read a book by a Hollywood screenwriter named Dalton Trumbo (jailed in the 1950s for refusing to talk to the House Committee on Un-American Activities about his political affiliations). The book was called *Johnny Got His Gun*. It is perhaps the most powerful antiwar novel ever written.

Here was war in its ultimate horror. A slab of flesh in an American uniform had been found on the battlefield, still alive, with no legs, no arms, no face, blind, deaf, unable to speak, but the heart still beating, the brain still functioning, able to think about his past, ponder his present condition, and wonder if he will ever be able to communicate with the world outside.

Around the same time I read a book by Walter Millis, *The Road to War,* which was an account of how the United States had been led into World War I by a series of lies and deceptions. Afterward I would learn more about those lies. For instance, the sinking of the ship *Lusitania* by German submarines was presented as a brutal, unprovoked act against a harmless passenger vessel. It was later revealed that the *Lusitania* was loaded with munitions intended for use against Germany; the ship's manifest had been falsified to hide that. This didn't lessen the ugliness of the sinking, but did show something about the ways in which nations are lured into war.

Class consciousness accounted for some of my feeling about war. I agreed with the judgment of the Roman biographer Plutarch, who said, "The poor go to war, to fight and die for the delights, riches, and superfluities of others."

It becomes difficult to sustain the claim that a war is just when both sides commit atrocities, unless one wants to argue that their atrocities are worse than ours. True, nothing done by the Allied Powers in World War II matches in utter viciousness the deliberate gassing, shooting, and burning of six million Jews and four million others by the Nazis. The deaths caused by the Allies were fewer, but still so massive as to throw doubt on the justice of a war that includes such acts.

Early in the war, various world leaders condemned the indiscriminate bombing of city populations. Italy had bombed civilians in Ethiopia; Japan, in China; Germany and Italy, in the Spanish Civil War. Germany had dropped bombs on Rotterdam in Holland, on Coventry in England and other places. Roosevelt described these bombings as "inhuman barbarism that has profoundly shocked the conscience of humanity."

But very soon, the United States and Britain were doing the same thing and on a far larger scale. When the Allied leaders met at Casablanca in January 1943, they agreed on massive air attacks to achieve "the destruction and dislocation of the German military, industrial and economic system and the undermining of the morale of the German people to the point where their capacity for armed resistance is fatally weakened." Churchill and his advisers had decided that bombing working-class districts of German cities would accomplish just that, "the undermining of the morale of the German people."

The saturation bombing of the German cities began. There were raids of a thousand planes on Cologne, Essen, Frankfurt, and Hamburg.

The British flew at night and did "area bombing" with no pretense of aiming at specific military targets.

The Americans flew in the daytime, pretending to precision, but bombing from high altitudes made that impossible. When I was doing my practice bombing in Deming, New Mexico, before going overseas, our egos were built up by having us fly at 4,000 feet and drop a bomb within twenty feet of the target. But at 11,000 feet, we were more likely to be 200 feet away. And when we flew combat missions, we did it from 30,000 feet, and might miss by a quarter of a mile. Hardly "precision bombing."

There was huge self-deception. We had been angered when the Germans bombed cities and killed several hundred or a thousand people. But now the British and Americans were killing tens of thousands in a single air strike. Michael Sherry, in his study of aerial bombing, notes that "so few in the air force asked questions." Sherry says there was no dear thinking about the effects of the bombing. Some generals objected, but were overruled by civilians. The technology crowded out moral considerations. Once the planes existed, targets had to be found.

It was terror bombing, and the German city of Dresden was the extreme example. (The city and the event are immortalized in fiction by Kurt Vonnegut's comic, bitter novel, *Slaughterhouse Five*.) It was February, 1945, the Red Army was eighty miles to the east and it was clear that Germany was on the way to defeat. In one day and one night of bombing, by American and British planes, the tremendous heat generated by the bombs created a vacuum, and an enormous firestorm swept the city, which was full of refugees at the time, increasing the population to a million. More than 100,000 people died.

The British pilot of a Lancaster bomber recalled, "There was a sea of fire covering in my estimation some forty square miles. We were so aghast at the awesome blaze that although alone over the city, we flew around in a stand-off position for many minutes before turning for home, quite subdued by our imagination of the horror that must be below."

By the time the atomic bomb was dropped on Hiroshima (August 6, 1945) and another on Nagasaki (three days later), the moral line had been crossed psychologically by the massive bombings in Europe and by the fire bombings of Tokyo and other cities.

The bomb on Hiroshima left perhaps 140,000 dead; the one on Nagasaki, 70,000 dead. Another 130,000 died in the next five years. Hundreds of thousands of others were left radiated and maimed. These numbers are based on the most detailed report that exists on the effects of the bombings; it was compiled by thirty-four Japanese specialists and was published in 1981.

The deception and self-deception that accompanied these atrocities was remarkable. Truman told the public, "The world will note that the first atomic bomb was dropped on Hiroshima, a military base. That was because we wished in this first attack to avoid, insofar as possible, the killing of civilians."

The terrible momentum of war continued even after the bombings of Hiroshima and Nagasaki. The end of the war was a few days away, yet B29s continued their missions. On August 14, five days after the Nagasaki bombing and the day before the actual acceptance of surrender terms, 449 B29s went out from the Marianas for a daylight strike and 372 more went out that night. Altogether, more than 1,000 planes were sent to bomb Japanese cities. There were no American losses. The last plane had not yet returned when Truman announced the Japanese had surrendered.

Japanese writer Oda Makoto describes that August 14 in Osaka, where he lived. He was a boy. He went out into the streets and found in the midst of the corpses American leaflets written in Japanese, which had been dropped with the bombs: Your government has surrendered; the war is over."

The American public, already conditioned to massive bombing, accepted the atomic bombings with equanimity, indeed with joy. I remember my own reaction. When the war ended in Europe, my crew flew our plane back to the United States. We were given a thirty-day furlough and then had to report for duty to be sent to Japan to continue bombing. My wife and I decided to spend that time in the countryside. Waiting for the bus to take us, I picked up the morning newspaper, August 7, 1945. The headline was "Atomic Bomb Dropped on Hiroshima." My immediate reaction was elation: "The war will end. I won't have to go to the Pacific."

I had no idea what the explosion of the atomic bomb had done to the men, women, and children of Hiroshima. It was abstract and distant, as were the deaths of the people from the bombs I had dropped in Europe from a height of six miles; I was unable to see anything below, there was no visible blood, and there were no audible screams. And I knew nothing of the imminence of a Japanese surrender. It was only later when I read John Hersey's *Hiroshima*, when I read the testimony of Japanese survivors, and when I studied the history of the decision to drop the bomb that I was outraged by what had been done.

Would it have been possible to trade time and territory for human life? Was there an alternative preferable to using the most modern weapons of destruction for mass annihilation? Can we try to imagine instead of a six-year war a ten-year or twenty-year period of resistance; of guerrilla warfare, strikes, and non-cooperation; of underground movements, sabotage, and paralysis of vital communication and transportation; and of clandestine propaganda for the organization of a larger and larger opposition?

Even in the midst of war, some nations occupied by the Nazis were able to resist: the Danes, the Norwegians, and the Bulgarians refused to give up their Jews. Gene Sharp, on the basis of his study of resistance movements in World War II, writes:

> During the second World War—in such occupied countries
> as the Netherlands, Norway and Denmark—patriots resisted
> their Nazi overlords and internal puppets by such weapons as
> underground newspapers, labor slowdowns, general strikes,
> refusal of collaboration, special boycotts of German troops
> and quislings, and non-cooperation with fascist controls and
> efforts to restructure their societies' institutions.

History is full of instances of successful resistance (although we are not informed very much about this) without violence and against tyranny, by people using strikes, boycotts, propaganda, and a dozen different ingenious forms of struggle. Gene Sharp, in his book *The Politics of Non-violent Action*, records hundreds of instances and dozens of methods of action.

Since the end of World War II, we have seen dictatorships overthrown by mass movements that mobilized so much popular opposition that the tyrant finally had to flee in Iran, in Nicaragua, in the Philippines, and in Haiti. Granted, the Nazi machine was formidable, efficient, and ruthless. But there are limits to conquest. A point is reached where the conqueror has swallowed too much territory, has to control too many people. Great empires have fallen when it was thought they would last forever.

We have seen, in the Eighties, mass movements of protest arise in the tightly controlled Communist countries of Eastern Europe, forcing dramatic changes in Hungary, Czechoslovakia, Poland, Bulgaria, Rumania, and East Germany. The Spanish people, having lost a million lives in their civil war, waited out Franco. He died, as all men do, and the dictatorship was over. For Portugal, the resistance in its outlying African Empire weakened control; corruption grew and the long dictatorship of Salazar was overthrown—without a bloodbath.

There was a famous "Milgram experiment" at Yale in the 1960s, named after the psychologist who supervised it. A group of paid volunteers were told that they were helping with an experiment dealing with the effects of punishment on learning. Each volunteer was seated in a position to observe someone taking a test, wearing electrodes connected to a control panel operated by the volunteer. The volunteer was told to monitor the test and, whenever a wrong answer was given, to pull a switch that would give a painful electrical jolt to the person taking the test, each wrong answer leading to a greater and greater electrical charge. There were thirty switches, with labels ranging from "Slight Shock" to "Danger—Severe Shock."

The volunteer was *not* told, however, that the person taking the test was an actor and that no real jolt was given. The actor would pretend to be in pain when the volunteer pulled the switch. When a volunteer became reluctant to continue causing pain, the experimenter in charge would say something like "The experiment requires that you continue." Under these conditions, two-thirds of the volunteers continued to pull the electrical switches on wrong answers, even when the subjects showed agonizing pain. One-third refused.

The experiment was tried with the volunteers at different distances from the subjects. When they were not physically close to the subject, about 35 percent of the volunteers defied authority even when they could not see or talk with the subject. But when they were right next to the subject, 70 percent refused the order.

The behavior of the people who were willing to inflict maximum pain can certainly be explained without recourse to "human nature." Their behavior was learned, not inborn. What they learned is what most people learn in modern culture, to follow orders, to do the job you are hired to do, to obey the experts in charge. In the experiment the supervisors, who had a certain standing and a certain legitimacy as directors of a "scientific" experiment, kept assuring the volunteers that they should go ahead, even if the subjects showed pain. When they were distant from the subjects, it was easier to obey the experimenters. But seeing or hearing the pain close up brought out some strong *natural* feeling of empathy, enough to disobey even the legitimate, confident, scientific supervisors of the experiment.

Some people interpreted the results of the experiment as showing an innate cruelty in human beings, but this was not the conclusion of Stanley Milgram, who directed the study. Milgram sums up his own views: "It is the extreme willingness of adults to go to almost any lengths on the command of an authority that constitutes the chief finding of the study . . . This is, perhaps, the most fundamental lesson of our study: ordinary people, simply doing their jobs, and without any particular hostility on their part, can become agents in a terrible destructive process."

So it is a learned response—"always obey," "do your job"—and not a natural drive, that caused so many of the people to keep pulling the pain switches. What is remarkable in the Milgram experiment, given the power of "duty . . . obedience" taught to us from childhood, is not that so many obeyed, but that so many refused.

C.P. Snow, a British novelist and scientist, wrote in 1961,

> When you think of the long and gloomy history of man, you will find more hideous crimes have been committed in the name of obedience than have ever been committed in the name of rebellion. The German Officer Corps were brought up in the most rigorous code of obedience . . . in the name of obedience they were party to, and assisted in, the most wicked large scale actions in the history of the world.

What about the evidence from anthropology—that is, from the behavior of "primitive" people, who are supposed to be closest to the "natural" state and, therefore, give strong clues about "human nature"? There have been many studies of the personality traits of such people: African Bushmen, North American Indians, Malay tribes, the Stone Age Tasaday from the Philippines, etc.

The findings can be summed up easily: There is no single pattern of warlike or peaceable behavior; the variations are very great. In North America, the Plains Indians were warlike, the Cherokee of Georgia were peaceful.

Anthropologist Colin Turnbull conducted two different studies in which he lived for a while with native tribes. In *The Forest People*, he describes the Pygmies of the Ituri rain forest in central Africa, wonderfully gentle and peaceful people whose idea of punishing a wrongdoer was to send him out into the forest to sulk. When he observed the Mbuti tribe of

Zaire, he found them cooperative and pacific. However, when Turnbull spent time with the Ik people of East Africa, whom he describes in *The Mountain People*, he found them ferocious and selfish.

The differences in behavior Turnbull found were explainable, not by genetics, not by the "nature" of these people, but by their environment, or their living conditions. The relatively easy life of the forest people fostered goodwill and generosity. The Ik, on the other hand, had been driven from their natural hunting grounds by the creation of a national game reserve into an isolated life of starvation in barren mountains. Their desperate attempt to survive brought out the aggressive destructiveness that Turnbull saw.

The men I knew in the air force—the pilots, navigators, bombardiers, and gunners on the crews flying over Europe, dropping bombs, and killing lots of people—were not lusting to kill, were not enthusiasts for violence, and were not war lovers. They—we—were engaged in large-scale killing, mostly of noncombatants, the women, children, and elderly people who happened to inhabit the neighborhoods of the cities that we bombed (officially, these were all "military targets"). But this did not come out of our natures, which were no different than when we were peacefully playing, studying, and living the lives of American boys back in Brooklyn, New York, or Aurora, Missouri.

The bloody deeds we did came out of a set of experiences not hard to figure out: We had been brought up to believe that our political leaders had good motives and could be trusted to do right in the world; we had learned that the world had good guys and bad guys, good countries and bad countries, and ours was good. We had been trained to fly planes, fire guns, operate bombsights, and to take pride in doing the job well. And we had been trained to follow orders, which there was no reason to question, because everyone on our side was good, and on the other side, bad. Besides, we didn't have to watch a little girl's legs get blown off by our bombs; we were 30,000 feet high and no human being on the ground was visible, no scream could be heard. Surely that is enough to explain how men can participate in war. We don't have to grope in the darkness of human nature.

While two million men served in Vietnam at one time or another, another half million evaded the draft in some way. And of those who served, there were perhaps 100,000 deserters. About 34,000 GIs were court-martialed and imprisoned. If an instinct really was at work, it was not for war, but against it.

Once in the war, the tensions of combat on top of the training in obedience produced atrocities. In the My Lai Massacre we have an extreme example of the power of a culture in teaching obedience. In My Lai, a hamlet in South Vietnam, a company of U.S. soldiers landed by helicopter early one morning in March 1968, with orders to kill everybody there. In about one hour, although not a single shot was fired at them, they slaughtered about 400 Vietnamese, most of them old people, women, and children. Many of them were herded into ditches and then mowed down with automatic rifles.

One of the American soldiers, Charles Hutto, said later, "The impression I got was that we was to shoot everyone in the village . . . An order came down to destroy all of the food, kill all the animals and kill all the people . . . then the village was burned . . . I didn't agree with the killings but we were ordered to do it."

It is not at all surprising that men go to war, when they have been cajoled, bribed, propagandized, conscripted, threatened, and also not surprising that after rigorous training they obey orders, even to kill unarmed women and children. What is surprising is that some refuse.

At My Lai a number of soldiers would not kill when ordered to: Michael Bernhardt, Roy Wood, Robert Maples, a GI named Grzesik. Warrant Officer Hugh Thompson commanded a helicopter that flew over the scene and, when he saw what was happening, he landed the helicopter and rescued some of the women and children, ordering his crewmen to fire on GIs if they fired on the Vietnamese. Charles Hutto, who participated in the My Lai Massacre, said afterward:

> I was 19 years old, and I'd always been told to do what the grown-ups told me to do . . . But now I'll tell my sons, if the government calls, to go, to serve their country, but to use their own judgment at times . . . to forget about authority . . . to use their own conscience.

CONCLUSION

Most young Americans know almost nothing about their country's relationship with the world. They know there's a war going on, they've heard about genocide in Africa, they have been told that Iran and China are threats to the United States. But ask them to provide some details and they return a blank stare.

It is understandable that today's youth, with so many entertainment options and electronic distractions, and with the pursuit of good times high on the list of priorities, can't be sufficiently aware of world issues. But they do read newspaper headlines and occasionally watch the news. They simply don't get enough information from these sources. If they hear at all about controversial issues, the information is oversimplified, incomplete, and often one-sided.

We've talked about values in this book, and the importance of looking beyond the illusions of war to seek an elusive reality. The values that we hold dear as Americans — honor, truth, self-awareness, compassion, altruism — are of little significance if we remain ignorant of the reasons for our wars and their effects on other people. Without that knowledge we cannot act in an appropriate manner. Without that knowledge we cannot act to improve our country, for we do not truly understand our failings. This accurate knowledge is, at the very least, what we can leave to our children before they become the leaders of our country.

They need to know that the U.S. is responsible for almost half of the world's total military expenditures, that nearly half of the arms sales to developing countries (in 2005) came from the United States, and that 20 of the top 25 recipients of U.S. arms sales in the developing world were declared undemocratic or human rights abusers by the U.S. State Department's own Human Rights Report.[1]

They need to know that the U.S. attempted to overthrow more than 40 foreign governments from the end of WW2 to the turn of the century, many of them populist and democratic movements that were battling oppressive regimes.[2]

They need to know that the U.S. went to war with Iraq in 2003 because of erroneous claims that Iraq possessed weapons of mass destruction and had ties to Al Qaeda.[3]

They need to know that studies by 16 U.S. intelligence agencies, including the CIA, the FBI, the State Dept., and all four branches of the armed forces, revealed that the occupation of Iraq has contributed to an increase in the overall terrorist threat. And that studies by the University of Chicago, the Hoover Digest, the Cato Institute, Iraq Body Count, and the 2005 Human Security Report support these findings.[4]

They need to know that the U.S. opposed United Nations votes on the right to food, the rights of women, the rights of children, and the right to freedom of people forcibly deprived of that right. That the U.S. opposed the banning of landmines. That the UN has accused the U.S. of repeatedly violating the World Convention against Torture, and that the UN voted the U.S. off the U.N. Human Rights Commission in 2001. And that at the end of 2006, eighty percent of the UN's unpaid dues were owed by the United States.[5]

They need to know that only eight corporations — Time Warner, Disney, Murdoch's News Corporation, Viacom (formerly CBS), General Electric, Yahoo, Google, and MSN — now control most of the U.S. media, and that some of them have close connections to companies making weaponry for the U.S. military.[6]

They need to know that while 3,000 Americans died in the horrible terrorist attack on September 11, 2001, every DAY of the year 30,000 children die of hunger and preventable diseases around the world. That the United Nations Human Development Report 2005 concluded that "The gap between the average citizen in the richest and in the poorest countries is wide and getting wider." That the World Bank's World Development Report 2006 stated that inequality in the U.S. is the worst in the developed world. That corporate income has risen much faster than workers' wages, while the corporate tax rate has dropped dramatically over the past 50 years.[7]

They need to know that U.S. foreign aid, based on percentage of income, is one of the lowest in the developed world. That much of our aid buys weaponry for relatively wealthy Israel. That 70% of U.S. aid is 'tied,' which means that the recipient must use it to purchase U.S. goods and services. That even our impressive level of private aid is mostly confined to donations within the U.S., and in the form of remittances (money sent back to the home countries of people working in the United States).[8]

They need to know that "free trade" can be an insidious form of economic warfare against developing countries. That we give more economic aid to our own multinational companies than foreign aid to poor countries. That U.S. tariffs on countries like Viet Nam and Bangladesh are 10 times higher than on European Union countries. That according to Christian Aid, trade liberalization in the past 20 years has cost sub-Saharan Africa more than $272 billion, a staggering sum that could have erased all its debts while paying for vaccination and school for every child. That the International Monetary Fund, the World Bank, the New Economics

Foundation, and the United Nations Report on the World Social Situation 2005 all reported that free trade has not helped the world's poor.[9]

Is it unpatriotic to criticize the behavior of one's own country? It depends on the meaning of patriotism. Socrates angered people by challenging them in public and exposing their ignorance. But he felt he was acting as a patriot by encouraging thoughtfulness over blind acceptance and celebration of government policies. In words attributed to him, "The unexamined life is not worth living." Like Socrates, Henry David Thoreau believed that citizens should tolerate nothing less from their government than the highest standards of behavior. He said, "Those who, while they disapprove of the character and measures of a government, yield to it their allegiance and support are undoubtedly its most conscientious supporters, and so frequently the most serious obstacles to reform."[10] Martin Luther King talked about moving "beyond the prophesying of smooth patriotism to the high grounds of a firm dissent based upon the mandates of conscience."[11]

But how do we know what's true and what isn't?

Opinions derived from any one source may be inaccurate, or biased, or simply wrong. Americans need to research the issues, to seek multiple sources if there's any question about the information available to them. That can be hard work. But it will teach us a lot about America's role in the world, and about the values that are important to us.

CONTRIBUTORS

Vic Blazier (Marion, OH) is an Iraq War veteran and active member of Iraq Veterans Against the War. He served in Iraq from April to November of 2003, and was awarded the Bronze Star Medal for his service.

Gayle Brandeis (Riverside, CA) is the author of Self Storage and The Book of Dead Birds, which won the Bellwether Prize for Fiction in Support of a Literature of Social Change. She is on the national staff of CODEPINK: Women for Peace.

Paul Buchheit (Chicago, IL) is a professor with Chicago City Colleges and the founder of Global Initiative Chicago (GIChicago.org), a consortium of universities and human rights organizations dedicated to promoting awareness of critical global issues.

Maurice Carney (Washington, DC) is the co-founder and Executive Director of the Friends of the Congo. He has worked as a research analyst at the Joint Center for Political and Economic Studies, an Africa working group coordinator for Reverend Jesse Jackson, and a research consultant to the Congressional Black Caucus Foundation.

Maureen Dolan is a Visiting Professor and Adjunct Interfaith Chaplain at DePaul University, teaching peace and justice courses as well as yoga and meditation. She is an ordained priest in the Kriya Yoga tradition and writes a regular column (as Swami Shraddhananda) for Yoga Chicago Magazine.

Tod Ensign (New York, NY) is an American veteran's rights lawyer and the Director of Citizen Soldier, a non-profit GI and veterans rights advocacy group which has 7,500 members nationwide.

María de Jesús Estrada, Ph.D. (Chicago, IL) was born into a farm-worker community in Yuma, Arizona. Jesú Estrada has been a longtime anti-poverty and equal rights activist, and was a key organizer in an anti-war walkout in Washington state. She is currently a professor of English in a Chicago city college, where she emphasizes peace studies. Jesú Estrada also sits on the editorial board of the Tribuno del Pueblo, a bilingual-anti poverty newspaper based out of Chicago.

Arun Gandhi (Rochester, NY), a grandson of India's late spiritual leader Mahatma Gandhi, is the founder and director of the M.K. Gandhi Institute for Nonviolence at Christian Brothers University, Memphis, Tennessee.

Tom H. Hastings (Portland, OR) is director of Peace & Nonviolence Studies track in the Conflict Resolution MA/MS program at Portland State University and author of: The Lessons of Nonviolence; Nonviolent Response to Terrorism; Ecology of War & Peace; Power; and Meek Ain't Weak: Nonviolent Power and People of Color.

Marc Herold (Durham, NH) is a professor of economics at the University of New Hampshire and the author of "Blown Away: The Myth and Reality of 'Precision Bombing' in Afghanistan."

Joshua Holland is a senior writer at AlterNet and contributes regularly to several blogs. He is also editor of AlterNet's corporate accountability and Iraq special coverage areas. Holland is the recipient of a Schumann Center for Media and Democracy writing grant for independent journalism.

Raed Jarrar (Washington, DC) is an political analyst and activist. He was born in Baghdad and spent most of his life in Iraq. Since August of 2006, Raed has worked towards bridging the gap between Iraqi leaders and U.S. Congress members. He is a member of the steering committee of the NY-based coalition United for Peace and Justice, and a consultant for the American Friends Service Committee.

Kathy Kelly (Chicago, IL) is an American peace activist, pacifist, three-time Nobel Peace Prize nominee and one of the founding members of Voices in the Wilderness.

Amy Meyers (Chicago, IL) is an active member of Vietnam Veterans Against the War (VVAW), Chicago Coalition Against War & Racism (CCAWR), and other social justice organizations. Her primary organizing efforts focus on anti-war issues, veteran support, and counter-recruitment.

Judi Nitsch (Chicago, IL) is an English professor with the Chicago City Colleges and an activist for human rights and women's rights.

Sherwood Ross is a Miami, Florida-based free-lance writer who covers military and political topics. He has worked as a reporter for the Chicago Daily News and several wire services and is a contributor to numerous national magazines.

Anup Shah (United Kingdom) has written and managed the globalissues.org web site since 1998. The site, which has a global audience and receives 50,000 page views daily, contains over 500 articles on critical world issues.

Cindy Sheehan (Crawford, TX) is an American anti-Iraq War activist, whose son, Casey Sheehan, was killed during his service in Iraq. She attracted international attention in August 2005 for her extended demonstration at a peace camp outside President George W. Bush's Texas ranch.

Ghada Talhami (Lake Forest, IL) is a professor of Middle East politics at Lake Forest College, where she holds the title of D.K.Pearsons Professor of Politics. She is the author of five books and is a frequent speaker on Arab, Palestinian, and Muslim issues.

Howard Zinn (Boston, MA) is an American historian, political scientist, social critic, activist and playwright, best known as author of the bestseller, *A People's History of the United States.*

ENDNOTES

Introduction

[1] Rampton, Sheldon. "No Shame." Center for Media and Democracy, 01/30/05 <http://prwatch.org/node/3220>. See also Damir Sagoljâ™s interview with Slovene magazine on June 21, 2004 at http://www.mladina.si/tednik/200425/clanek/sve-intervju—gregor_cerar/; also "Linda Eddy, Propaganda Poster Artist, Replies." Daily Kos, Feb 04, 2005 <http://www.dailykos.com/story/2005/2/4/233054/8970>; and Source Watch, "Iowa Presidential Watch." July 1, 2007 <http://www.sourcewatch.org/index.php?title=Iowa_Presidential_Watch>.

Honor
Illusion 1: We fight for peace and democracy

[1] Kagan, Robert. *Dangerous Nation: America's Place in the World from Its Earliest Days to the Dawn of the Twentieth Century. Knopf*, 2006. See also Kinzer, Stephen. *Overthrow: America's Century of Regime Change from Hawaii to Iraq.* Henry Holt & Co., 2006.

[2] Graymont, Barbara. *The Iroquois in the American Revolution.* Syracuse, NY: Syracuse University Press, 1972.

[3] U.S. Department of State. "Monroe Doctrine." <http://www.state.gov/r/pa/ho/time/jd/16321.htm>

[4] "Our Enemies and U.S.," cited by Ido Oren. *Atlantic Monthly* 1901. Cornell 2002. See also Powell, Jim. "U.S. Has Long History of Waging Wrong Wars." 2 Jun 2005. CATO Institute. <http://www.foxnews.com/story/0,2933,157970,00html>

[5] U.S. Interventions in Latin America Since 1823 <http://www.mindfully.org/Reform/2003/US-Interventions-1823.htm>

[6] Cooperative Research <http://www.cooperativeresearch.org/context.jsp?item+USDOSMemoSaudiOisisPrize>

[7] Mitchell, Luke. "Blood for Oil." *Harper's Magazine.* 2004.

[8] Tyler, Patrick. "U.S. Strategy Plan Calls for Insuring No Rivals Develop." *The New York Times*, 8 March 1992.

[9] Barash, David P. and Webel, Charles P. *Peace and Conflict Studies.* Sage Publications, 2002.

[10] Grossman, Zoltan. "From Wounded Knee to Afghanistan: A Century of US Military Interventions." Evergreen State College, Accessed July 2007. See also Blum, William. "A Brief History of U.S. Interventions: 1945 to the Present." *Z Magazine*, June 1999.

[11] Kinzer, "Overthrow," op. cit.

[12] Schlesinger, Stephen and Stephen Kinzer. "Bitter Fruit: The Story of the American Coup in Guatemala". Harvard University. David Rockefeller Center for Latin American Studies, 2005. See also Babingston, Charles. "Clinton: Support for Guatemala Was Wrong". Washington Post. March 11, 1999. <http://www.washingtonpost.com/wp-srv/inatl/daily/march99/clinton11.htm>

[13] Spartacus Educational. Rafael Trujillo. <http://www.spartacus.schoolnet.co.uk/JFKtrujillo.htm> See also Solomon, Norman. *War Made Easy.* John Wiley & Sons, 2005; Blum, William. *Killing Hope.* Common Courage Press, 1995 & 2003 http://www.lossless-audio.com/usa/index0.php?page=786588780.htm

[14] "US-Chile (1964-2005), Project: History of US Interventions" <http://www.cooperativeresearch.org/timeline.jsp?timeline=chile> See also Bernstein, Dennis and Sydel, Laura. "Dictators Supported by the U.S. Government". From "Friendly

165

Dictators" 1995 <http://www.omnicenter.org/warpeacecollection/dictators.htm> ; National Security Archive Electronic Briefing Book No. 8, September 2001; No. 110, February 2004; Kornbluh, Peter. "CIA Acknowledges Ties to Pinochet's Repression," National Security Archive. Chile Documentation Project, 19 Sep. 2000. <http:// www.gwu.edu/~nsarchiv/news/20000919>

[15] Solomon, Norman. *War Made Easy*. op. cit. See also "Report Alleges US Role in Angola Arms-for-Oil Scandal," by Wayne Madsen, Special to CorpWatch, May 17th, 2002 (http://www.corpwatch.org/article.php?id=2576)

[16] "Nicaragua's New Constitution." *World Policy Journal* (Vol 4,No 2), Spring 1987. See also Melrose, Dianna. The Threat of a Good Example. Oxford, UK: Oxfam, 1985; Timeline: Nicaragua <http://www.stanford.edu/group/arts/nicaragua/discovery_eng/ timeline>; "Military and Paramilitary Activities in and Against Nicaragua," International Court of Justice, 27 June 1986. Security Council S/18221, 11 July 1986; Franklin, Charles H. "Presidential Approval in Perspective." University of Wisconsin, Madison, May 2003.

[17] Wilentz, Amy. "Coup in Haiti." *The Nation*, 4 Mar 2004. See also Farmer, Paul. Pathologies of Power. University of California Press, 2005; Shah, Anup. "Haiti and Human Rights." 19 Jun 2004. <http://www.globalissues.org/HumanRights/Abuses/ Haiti.asp> Cohn, Marjorie. "US Pulls the Strings in Haiti." Truthout. 09/29/05 <http://www.globalpolicy.org/security/issues/haiti/2005/0929us.htm>.

[18] Smith, Michael. "The War before the War." *New Statesman*, 30 May 2005. See also "Why Did Attorney General Support Such a Weak and Dismal Argument?" The Guardian. 23 Feb 2005; Shane, Scott. "Ex-C.I.A. Official Says Iraq Data Was Distorted." New York Times, 11 Feb 2006; "The Downing Street Memo(s)." <http:/ /www.downingstreet memo.com>

[19] Henderson, Errol. *Democracy and War: The End of an Illusion?* Lynne Rienner Publications 2002. See also Barkawi, Tarak. *Globalization and War*. Rowman and Littlefield, 2006; Barbieri, Katherine. *The Liberal Illusion: Does Trade Promote Peace?* University of Michigan Press, 2002.

[20] "Israel 3rd From Bottom on Global Peace Index," Ynet and AP News, 31 May 2007. <http://www.ynetnews.com/articles/0,7340,L-3406941,00.html>

[21] The Human Security Report 2005 <www.humansecurityreport.info>. See also the Human Development Report 2005 (Chapter 5) <http://hdr.undp.org/reports/global/ 2005>; and Grossman, Zoltan op. cit.

[22] "Active Duty Military Personnel Strengths by Regional Area and by Country," Dept. of Defense, 31 Dec. 2004. See also "Base Structure Report," Department of Defense, FY 2006; Vance, Laurence M. "The Burden of Empire," 18 Mar 2004 <http:// www.countercurrents.org/us-vance180304.htm> ; Monthly Review, 2002 <http:// www.globalpolicy.org/empire/intervention/2003/0710imperialmap.htm>

[23] SIPRI Yearbook 2006. Stockholm International Peace Research Institute. See also "World Wide Military Expenditures" <http://www.globalsecurity.org/military/world/ spending.htm>; "U.S. Military Spending vs. the World," Center for Arms Control and Non-Proliferation, 5 Feb 2007 <http://www.armscontrolcenter.org/archives/ 002279.php>; Shah, Anup "World Military Spending." February 25, 2007 <http:// www.globalissues.org/Geopolitics/ArmsTrade/Spending.asp>

[24] Eight Hiroshima bombs = 8 x 15 kilotons (120 kilotons); U.S. arsenal is 1200 megatons (1,200,000 kilotons); Russia has an approximately equivalent nuclear arsenal. Graphic inspired by Ben Cohen, May 2005 <http://www.truemajority.org/ bensbbs>. See also Table of US Strategic Nuclear Forces 2002, Archive of Nuclear Data, Natural Resources Defense Council; United States Nuclear Forces 2005, Carnegie Endowment for International Peace; Global nuclear stockpiles 1945-2006, Bulletin of the Atomic Scientists; Turco, R.P., Toon, O.B., Ackerman, T.P., Pollack, J.B.,

Sagan, Carl. "Nuclear Winter: Global Consequences of Multiple Nuclear Explosions", *Science*, V. 222, No 4630, December 23, 1983.

[25] "FACTBOX: Highlights of Bush's Fiscal 2008 Budget," Reuters, 5 Feb 2007. See also "Bush Sends $2.9 Trillion Budget to Congress," Associated Press, 5 Feb 2007.

[26] Nordhaus William D. "The Cost of the Iraq War Put in Perspective." Baltimore Chronicle, 19 Sep 2003. See also "Iraq Costs Said to Hit $320 Bln, Then Double Before War Ends." Bloomberg, 27 Apr 2006.

[27] Eland, Ivan. "Wasting Billions on Military Spending." The Independent Institute, 5 Feb 2007.

[28] "A Unified Security Budget for the United States 2006." Center for Defense Information: Foreign Policy In Focus, May 2005 <www.fpif.org/pdf/reports/USB.pdf>

[29] "Weaponeers of Waste: A Critical Look at the Bush Administration Energy Department's Nuclear Weapons Complex and the First Decade of Science-Based Stockpile Stewardship," Apr 2004 <http://www.nrdc.org/nuclear/weaponeers/contents.asp>

[30] "China to Increase Military Spending: China to Increase its 2007 Military Budget by 17.8 Percent to Nearly $45 Billion." CBS News, WBBM, Chicago, 4 Mar 2007.

[31] Dolgov, Anna. "Russian Exercises Flex Military Muscle," Boston Globe, 21 Feb 2004. See also Chomsky, Noam. *Hegemony or Survival*. Henry Holt & Co., 2003-2004.

[32] Isachenkov,Vladimir. "Putin: 'U.S. has Triggered New Arms Race'". Associated Press. 31 May 2007

[33] "Conventional Arms Transfers to Developing Nations, 1998-2005." CRS Report for Congress, 23 Oct 2006 <http://www.fas.org/sgp/crs/weapons/RL33696.pdf>

[34] Berrigan, Frida and Hartung, William D. with Heffel, Leslie. "U.S. Weapons at War 2005: Promoting Freedom or Fueling Conflict?" June 2005. See also "FOCUS: Selling Weapons to the World." 10 Jun 2005 <http://www.newsdesk.org/archives/000205.php>; "The G8: Global Arms Exporters: Failing to Prevent Irresponsible Arms Transfers" Amnesty International, IANSA, Oxfam International, June 2005

[35] Berrigan, Frida. "U.S. Leads the World in Sale of Military Goods." Foreign Policy in Focus, 3 Oct 2005 <http://www.fpif.org/fpiftxt/1284>. See also "FOCUS: Selling Weapons to the World," 10 Jun 2005 <http://www.newsdesk.org/archives/000205.php>

[36] Caldicott, Helen. *The New Nuclear Danger*. New York: The New Press, 2002.

[37] Hartung, William D. "Mercenaries, Inc. How a U.S. Company Props Up the House of Saud." *The Progressive*, April 1996.

[38] "Small Arms and Conflict in West Africa: Testimony of Lisa Misol, Human Rights Watch Researcher, Before the Congressional Human Rights Caucus." May 20, 2004. See also "Conventional Arms Transfers to Developing Nations, 1997-2004," Congressional Research Service, The Library of Congress, August 29, 2005; Sullivan, Robert E. "Burgeoning Small Arms Trade Has High Profits and Losses." *Earth Times*, March 2001.

[39] "Iraq's Arms Bazaar." *Newsweek*, August 27, 2007.

[40] Snyder, Jack and Mansfield, Edward. "Democratization and the Danger of War". International Security 20, no. 1. 1995

[41] Horowitz, Donald. "Democracy in Divided Societies" Johns Hopkins University Press. 1994. See also Rabushka, Alvin and Kenneth Shepsle. "Politics in Plural Societies: A Theory of Democratic Instability". Charles E. Merill. 1972

[42] "Democracy's Dilemmas." *The Nation*, March 10, 2005.

[43] "A Year After Iraq War," Summary of Findings, Pew Research Center for the People & the Press, March 16, 2004.

[44] "World View of US Role Goes From Bad to Worse". BBC World Service Poll. January 23, 2007. See also "Trends in Public Opinion about the War in Iraq, 2003-2007". Pew Research Center. March 15, 2007.

45 "The Pew Global Attitudes Project: Global Unease with Major World Powers", June 27, 2007 <http://pewglobal.org/reports/pdf/256.pdf>

46 "America's Image in the World: Findings from the Pew Global Attitudes Project". Pew Global Attitudes Project, March 14, 2007 <http://pewglobal.org/commentary/display.php?AnalysisID=1019>

47 Rampton, Sheldon & Stauber, John. *Weapons of Mass Deception*. Penguin. 2003

48 Butler, Smedley. *War is a Racket*. Round Table Press, 1935.

49 Verlöy, André and Daniel Politi. "Advisors of Influence: Nine Members of the Defense Policy Board Have Ties to Defense Contractors." Data by Aron Pilhofer. March 28, 2003 <http://publicintegrity.org/report.aspx?aid=91&sid=200>.

50 Department of Defense, Office of Reconstruction and Humanitarian Assistance, New York Times, 7 May 2003. Chart shown in *The New York Times*, 7 May 2003; Source: Department of Defense, Office of Reconstruction and Humanitarian Assistance.

51 "Executive Excess 2006." Institute for Policy Studies and United for a Fair Economy, 2006

52 "Three Years in Iraq," Halliburton Watch, accessed August 2007 <halliburtonwatch.org>

53 Turnipseed, Tom. "Dick Cheney: War Profiteer." CommonDreams.org, November 17, 2005.

54 Rosen, Ruth. "As Ordered, It's About Oil." *San Francisco Chronicle*, August 8, 2003.

55 "Goodbye Houston: An Alternative Annual Report on Halliburton." CorpWatch, May 15th, 2007.

56 "Halliburton's Dubai Move Sparks Outcry." CBS News, DUBAI, United Arab Emirates. March 12, 2007

57 "Bechtel: Profiting from Destruction." CorpWatch, Global Exchange, Public Citizen, Collaborative Report, June 5th, 2003. See also Juhasz, Antonia. "Bechtel Takes a Hit for War Profiteering." AlterNet, August 4, 2006.

58 Cray, Charlie. "The 10 Most Brazen War Profiteers." Center for Corporate Policy, AlterNet, September 5, 2006. <http://www.alternet.org/waroniraq/41083>

59 Caldicott, op. cit. See also "Collateral Damage." *The Economist*, August 26, 2006.

60 "Top 100 Federal Prime Contractors." <http://www.washingtontechnology.com/top-100/2007>

61 Weiner, Tim. "Lockheed and the Future of Warfare." *The New York Times*, November 28, 2004.

62 "Pentagon Allows Export of US Navy's Newest Jet US in arms race with itself." Council for a livable world, Arms Trade Insider, August 9, 2001. <http://www.clw.org/archive/atop/inside/inside51.html>

63 Shanahan, Vice Admiral Jack, Commander, NATO Strike Fleet (ret.); Director, Center for Defense Information <http://academic.regis.edu/jroth/ARMS%20FOR%20THE%20POOR.htm>

64 Johnson, Chalmers. *Blowback*. Henry Holt & Co., 2000,2004. See also St. Clair, Jeffrey. *Grand Theft Pentagon*. Common Courage Press, 2005.

65 Friends Committee on National Legislation, Washington Newsletter, March 2006.

66 Fact Sheet on the JSF F-35. Center for Defense Information. August 6, 2007 <http://www.cdi.org/program/document.cfm?DocumentID=4055>

67 Kennedy, Sean. "Joint Strike Fighter is Latest Abuse of Emergency Funding." Citizens Against Government Waste, January 24, 2007.

68 Berrigan, Frida. "A Nation of Firsts Arms the World." World Policy Institute, May 21, 2007 <http://www.commondreams.org/archive/2007/05/18/1333>. See also "Global Unease With Major World Powers." Pew Global Attitudes Project, June 27, 2007.

69   Pringle, Evelyn. "Bush Family War Profiteering." Counterpunch, April 12, 2007
      <http://counterpunch.org/pringle04122007.html>.
70   The MIPT Terrorism Knowledge Base. Accessed August, 2007. <http://www.tkb.org>
71   Bergen, Peter and Cruickshank, Paul. "The Iraq Effect: War Has Increased Terrorism
      Sevenfold Worldwide." Mother Jones, March 1, 2007.
72   "Year Four: Simply the worst," Press release 15: Iraq Body Count March 18th 2007
      <http://www.iraqbodycount.org/press/pr15.php>. See also "Bombings are deadliest
      since Iraq war began." Associated Press. Aug 15, 2007 <http://www.msnbc.msn.com/
      id/20274765/?GT1=10252>.
73   Pape, Robert A. "Suicide Terrorism and Democracy: What We've Learned Since 9/
      11." Cato Institute, September 8, 2006 <http://www.cato.org/
      event.php?eventid=3063>.
74   "Hatred of U.S. drives al-Qaida recruiting." NBC News, 10/16/07.
75   "Spy agencies: Terror threat grows," New York Times News Service, September 24,
      2006. See also "Stating the obvious." The Economist, September 30 2006.
76   Zuckerman, Mortimer B. "Getting Serious About Oil." US News & World Report,
      August 7, 2006 <http://www.usnews.com/usnews/opinion/articles/060730/7edit.htm>.

Illusion 2: We fight to defend our personal freedoms

1   American Civil Liberties Union. "Arresting Protest: A Special Report of the New
      York Civil Liberties Union on New York City's Protest Policies at the February 15,
      2003 Antiwar Demonstration in New York City." 23 Apr. 2003. <www.nyclu.org/
      arresting_protest_042803.html>.
2   The Associated Press ran a 330-word story mentioning "over 300 protestors" at the
      rush hour Times Square protest, organized that day by A.N.S.W.E.R. A story with
      twice the word count ran on the same day, detailing the militarizing of NYPD in the
      face is potential 'terror.'
3   Ferguson, Sarah. "It's On: Where and How to Protest in New York." The Village
      Voice. 20 Mar. 2003. 01 Jun. 2007 <http://www.villagevoice.com/news/
      0313,ferguson,42794,6.html>.
4   Fairness and Accuracy In Reporting. "NPR, New York Times Count Out Anti-War
      Activists." FAIR. 28 Oct. 2003 <http://www.fair.org/index.php?page=2490>. See
      also Fairness and Accuracy in Reporting. "Times, NPR Change Their Take on DC
      Protests," FAIR 30 Oct. 2003. <http://www.fair.org/index.php?page=1640>.
5   Whiten, Jon. "Does Size Really Matter? Analyzing the Press's Protest Coverage."
      Extra! Jul./Aug 2005 <http://www.fair.org/index.php?page=2628>. The article
      waited until much later in the story to give a more complete picture of the protests'
      size, noting in the 11th paragraph that 'several thousand protesters marched from
      Harlem to Central Park.' In the 15th paragraph, we learn that 'it seemed likely that
      tens of thousands took part across America.'
6   Rendall, Steve & Broughel, Tara. "Amplifying Officials, Squelching Dissent: Fair
      Study Finds Democracy Poorly Served by War Coverage." Extra! May/Jun. 2003
      <http://www.fair.org/index.php?page=1145>.
7   ibid. Of U.S. employees, military personnel comprised 68 percent of U.S. official
      sources and 47 percent of all U.S. sources.
8   ibid. Rendall and Broughel offered the following range of major network broadcasting
      of antiwar voices: "4 percent at NBC, 3 percent at CNN, ABC, PBS and FOX, and
      less than 1 percent — one out of 205 U.S. sources — at CBS."
9   Bulletin's Frontrunner. 7 Apr. 2003. LexisNexis. Indiana U Library. Bloomington,
      IN. 01 Jun. 2007 <http://bert.lib.indiana.edu:2091/universe/>.
10   United for Peace and Justice. About United for Peace and Justice. 01 Jun 2007 <http:/
      /www.unitedforpeace.org/article.php?list=type&type=16>.

[11]   American Civil Liberties Union. "Freedom Under Fire: Dissent in Post 9/11 America." May 2003. <http://www.aclu.org/safefree/resources>. See also American Civil Liberties Union. "No Real Threat: The Pentagon's Secret Database on Peaceful Protest." Jan. 2007 <http://www.aclu.org/safefree/resources>; American Civil Liberties Union. "The Surveillance-Industrial Complex: How the American Government Is Conscripting Businesses and Individuals in the Construction of a Surveillance Society." Aug. 2004 <http://www.aclu.org/safefree/resources>.

[12]   American Civil Liberties Union. "ACLU Denounces FBI Tactics Targeting Political Protesters." 16 Aug. 2004. <http://www.aclu.org/safefree/spying/18514prs 20040816.html>. See also American Civil Liberties Union. "ACLU Slams Classified FBI Memorandum Directing Law Enforcement to Engage in Protest Suppression Tactics." 23 Nov. 2003. <http://www.aclu.org/safefree/general/16960prs 20031123.html>.

[13]   Forbes, Daniel. "Operation Atlas." AlterNet. 17 Sep. 2003. < http://www.alternet.org/rights/16772/>

[14]   Weissenstein, Michael. "Changed Police Department on Guard Against Terror." Associated Press. 20 Mar. 2003. LexisNexis. Indiana U Library. Bloomington, IN. <http://bert.lib.indiana.edu:2091/universe/>.

[15]   American Civil Liberties Union. "No Real Threat.." op. cit. The ACLU includes the FIOA-procured documents of 30 groups deemed "non-credible" threats to U.S. security.

[16]   American Civil Liberties Union. "ACLU Denounces.." "ACLU Slams.." op. cit. See also American Civil Liberties Union. "City Cannot Block Release of NYPF Materials from Republican National Convention, Federal Court Rules." 22 Jan. 2007 <http://www.aclu.org/freespeech/protest/28120prs20070122.html>; Dunn, Christopher, et al. "Rights and Wrongs at the RNC: A Special Report about Police and Protest at the Republican National Convention." 2005. < http://www.nyclu.org/pdfs/rnc_report_083005.pdf>; Spying on the Home Front. 2007. PBS Online. <http://www.pbs.org/wgbh/pages/frontline/homefront/view/>. This report details government-corporate collusion in massive "data sweep" operations, as federal law enforcement agencies mine commercial data banks for consumer data on millions of Americans.

Truthfulness
Illusion 3: Our government tells us the truth about war

[1]   Native Americans of North America, MSN Encarta

[2]   Mexican-American War, MSN Encarta

[3]   Abraham Lincoln Spot Resolution, MSN Encarta

[4]   Misperceptions, the Media and the Iraq War. The PIPA/Knowledge Networks Poll, Program on International Policy Attitudes. October 2, 2003 <http://65.109.167.118/pipa/pdf/oct03/IraqMedia_Oct03_rpt.pdf>.

[5]   Butler, Smedley. *War is a Racket*. Round Table Press, 1935.

[6]   Trumbo, Dalton. *Johnny Got His Gun*. Bantam Books, 1938.

[7]   Gregory, Anthony. Sixty-Three Years of Lies. <http://www.strike-the-root.com/4/gregory/gregory27.html>

[8]   Stinnett, Robert B. "December 7, 1941: A Setup from the Beginning." Honolulu Advertiser, December 7, 2000, cited at <http://www.independent.org/newsroom/article.asp?id=103>.

[9]   Bradlee, Ben. Deceit in American Government: Gulf of Tonkin. <http://www.the7thfire.com/Politics%20and%20History/Gulf-of-Tonkin.htm>.

Illusion 4: We stay in Iraq to prevent further bloodshed among Iraqis

[1] Jarrar, Raed and Holland, Joshua. "Majority of Iraqi Lawmakers Now Reject Occupation". AlterNet. May 9, 2007.

[2] Jarrar, Raed. "The Four Missing Points" In the Middle. July 2, 2006 <http://raedinthemiddle.blogspot.com/2006/07/four-missing-points.html>

[3] "Yankee, Go Home." Anti-War.com. April 11, 2007.

[4] Cole, Juan. "Informed Comment: Thoughts on the Middle East, History, and Religion." President of the Global Americana Institute. July 30, 2005.

[5] Dreyfuss, Robert. "Bush's Meeting With A Murderer". TomPaine.com. December 04, 2006.

Illusion 5: The mainstream media gives us balanced reporting

[1] Cornog, Evan, 'Let's Blame the Readers', *Columbia Journalism Review*, Issue1, January/February 2005, (last accessed April 27, 2007) <http://www.cjr.org/issues/2005/1/cornog-readers.asp>

[2] Engel, Matthew, 'US media cowed by patriotic fever, says CBS star', *Guardian Unlimited*, [London], May 17, 2002, (last accessed May 19, 2007), <http://www.guardian.co.uk/bush/story/0,7369,717097,00.html>.

[3] Terdiman, Daniel, "Dan Rather: Journalism has 'lost its guts', *CNET News.com*, March 12, 2007, (last accessed May 19, 2007). <http://news.com.com/2100-1025_3-6166528.html>

[4] 'And then there were eight: 25 years of media mergers, from GE-NBC to Google-YouTube', *Mother Jones*, March 2007, (last accessed April 27, 2007). <http://www.motherjones.com/news/feature/2007/03/and then_there_were_eight.pdf>

[5] Guiterrez, Miren, 'Fewer players, less freedom', Inter Press Service, March 20, 2004, <http://www.ipsnews.net/interna.asp?idnews=22950>

[6] Bagdikian, Ben H., *The Media Monopoly*, Boston: Beacon Press, Sixth Edition, 2000. See also McChesney, Robert, *Rich Media Poor Democracy*, Illinois: University of Illinois Press, 1999.

[7] 'FCC Destroyed Media Ownership Report; Study found local ownership means more local news', *Fairness and Accuracy In Reporting*, September 9, 2006 <http://www.fair.org/index.php?page=2960>. See also "Review of the Radio Industry", FCC Media Bureau, 2004, <http://www.stopbigmedia.com/files/radio_ownership.pdf>

[8] Talbot, Karen, 'Backing up Globalization with Military Might', *Covert Action Quarterly*, Issue 68, Fall 1999, <http://www.globalissues.org/Geopolitics/Articles/Backing.asp>

[9] Smith, J.W, *Economic Democracy: The Political Struggle for the 21ˢᵗ Century*, 4ᵗʰ Edition, Cambria: Institute for Economic Democracy Press, 2005

[10] Shah, Anup, 'Bush Doctrine of Preemptive Strikes; A Global Pax Americana', *Global Issues*, April 24, 2004, <http://www.globalissues.org/Geopolitics/Empire/Bush.asp>

[11] Chomsky, Noam, *The Common Good*, Boston: Odonian Press, 1998

[12] Nichols, John, 'Newspapers...and After?', *The Nation*, January 29, 2007 issue, <http://www.thenation.com/doc/20070129/nichols>. See also Turner, Derek, 'Out of The Picture: Minority & Female TV Station Ownership in the United States', *freepress.net*, October 2006 <http://www.stopbigmedia.com/files/out_of_the_picture.pdf>; "Locked Out: The Lack of Gender and Ethnic Diversity on Cable News Continues", Media Matters, May 7, 2007, <http://mediamatters.org/items/200705070003>; "Sunday Shutout: The Lack of Gender & Ethnic Diversity on the Sunday Morning Talk Shows." Media Matters, May 14, 2007, <http://mediamatters.org/items/200705140001>

[13] Farsetta, Diane and Price, Daniel, 'Fake TV News: Widespread and Undisclosed', Center for Media and Democracy, April 6, 2006, <http://www.prwatch.org/fakenews/

execsummary> See also Miller, David, 'The Age of the Fake', *Spin Watch*, March 14, 2005, <http://www.spinwatch.org/content/view/128/8/>.

[14] Barstow, David and Stein, Robin, 'Under Bush, a New Age of Prepackaged TV News', *The New York Times*, March 13, 2005, <http://www.nytimes.com/2005/03/13/politics/13covert.html>

[15] Thom Shanker and Eric Schmitt, "Pentagon Weighs Use of Deception in a Broad Arena", *The New York Times*, December 13, 2004.

[16] Kelley, Matt, 'Pentagon Rolls Out Stealth PR', USA Today, December 14, 2005, <http://www.usatoday.com/news/washington/2005-12-14-pentagon-pr_x.htm>

[17] MediaLens, 'Pentagon Propaganda Occupies Guardian's Front Page', *MediaLens*, May 24, 2007, <http://www.medialens.org/alerts/07/070524_pentagon_propaganda_occupies.php>

[18] Smith, J.W., op. cit.

[19] Pilger, John, 'In the freest press on earth, humanity is reported in terms of its usefulness to US power', *New Statesman*, February 19, 2001, <http://www.newstatesman.com/200102190008>

[20] 'Marketing Tomorrow's Weapons', Center for Defense Information, first broadcast September 1997, <http://www.cdi.org/adm/transcripts/1103/>

[21] Campbell, Duncan, 'Top Gun versus Sergeant Bilko? No contest, says the Pentagon', *The Guardian*, August 29, 2001, <http://film.guardian.co.uk/News_Story/Guardian/0,4029,543821,00.html>

[22] Cohen, Jeff and Solomon, Norman, 'Tonkin Gulf Lie Launched Vietnam War', Media Beat, July 27, 1994, <http://www.fair.org/index.php?page=2261>. See also Pilger, John. *Heroes*, London: Vintage, 2001

[23] Knightley, Phillip, *The First Casualty: The War Correspondent as Hero, Propagandist and Myth-Maker*, London: Andre Deutsch Ltd (1975, revised 2003)

[24] Smith, J.W., op. cit.

[25] Blum, William, *Rogue State*. Common Courage Press, 2000

[26] Peterson, Scott, 'In war, some facts less factual', *Christian Science Monitor*, September 6, 2002 <http://www.csmonitor.com/2002/0906/p01s02-wosc.html>. See also Urbina, Ian, 'This War Brought to You by Rendon Group', *Asia Times*, November 14, 2002, <http://www.gvnews.net/html/Shadow/alert3553.html>

[27] This was reported by *Business Week* and others later in 2003 after the second assault on Iraq, but it certainly did not make prime time headlines.

[28] Shah, Anup. 'Iraq: Effects of Sanctions', Global Issues, October 2, 2005, <http://www.globalissues.org/Geopolitics/MiddleEast/Iraq/Sanctions.asp>

[29] Shah, Anup. 'Iraq war aftermath: Media Reporting, Journalism and Propaganda; Civilian Casualties', Global Issues, May 7, 2007, <http://www.globalissues.org/Geopolitics/MiddleEast/Iraq/PostWar/Media.asp#CivilianCasualties>

[30] Mayer, Jane, 'The Manipulator', *The New Yorker*, May 29, 2004, <http://www.newyorker.com/archive/2004/06/07/040607fa_fact1>

[31] Hollar, Julie and Peter Hart. "When "Old News" Has Never Been Told". July/August 2005. <http://www.fair.org/index.php?page=2612>. See also "Why Did Attorney General Support Such a Weak and Dismal Argument?". *The Guardian*. February 23, 2005. <http://politics.guardian.co.uk/iraq/story/0,12956,1423230,00.html>; "Book: Bush, Blair were set on Iraq war despite UN". *Chicago Tribune*. February 11, 2006.

[32] "Saving Private Lynch story 'flawed'". BBC. May 15, 2003. <http://news.bbc.co.uk/1/hi/programmes/correspondent/3028585.stm>; See also Whitelaw, Kevin. "Selling A Convenient Untruth". *US News & World Report*, April 29, 2007.

[33] "Annual Terror Report Won't Include Numbers." *Washington Post*. April 19, 2005. See also Landay, Jonathan S. "U.S. eliminates annual terrorism report". Knight Ridder Newspapers. April 16, 2005. <http://seattletimes.nwsource.com/html/nationworld/2002243262_terror16.html>

[34]   "Iran: U.S. Concerns and Policy Responses". CRS Report for Congress. January 5, 2007. <http://fpc.state.gov/documents/organization/78547.pdf>

[35]   '2007 Worldwide Press Freedom Index', *Reporters Without Borders*, October 2007, <http://www.rsf.org/article.php3?id_article=24022>

Self-Awareness

[1]   Hedges, Chris. *War Is a Force That Gives Us Meaning.* Anchor Books, 2002.

[2]   Johnson, Dominic. "Do Positive Illusions Promote War?" Harvard University, 2003.

Illusion 6: War Doesn't Impact Me Personally

[1]   <http://www.costofwar.org>

[2]   <http://www.josephstiglitz.com>

[3]   The National Priorities Project. <http://www.nationalpriorities.org>

[4]   See "A Vote for More War: States and Congressional Districts." <http://www.nationalpriorities.org/Publications/A-Vote-for-More-War-States-and-Congressional-Dist-2.html>.

[5]   Barash, David, ed. *Approaches to Peace.* New York: Oxford UP, 2000.

[6]   The Peace Alliance. <http://www.britshalom.org>

[7]   Iraq Veterans Against the War. <http://www.ivaw.org>

[8]   Appeal for Redress. <http://appealforredress.org>

[9]   Thank You Lt. Ehren Watada. <http://thankyoult.org>.

[10]   Sussman, Dalia. "Poll Shows View of Iraq War is Most Negative Since Start." New York Times, 25 May 2007

[11]   Intergovernmental Panel on Climate Change. <http://www.ipcc.ch>

[12]   Doomsday Clock. The Bulletin Online. <http://thebulletin.org>

[13]   Pape, Robert A.. *Dying to Win: The Strategic Logic of Suicide Terrorism.* New York: Random House, 2005.

[14]   Klare, Michael T. *Blood and Oil: The Dangers and Consequences of America's Growing Dependency on Imported Petroleum.* New York: Henry Holt, 2004.

[15]   "Updated Iraq Survey Affirms Earlier Mortality Estimates," Johns Hopkins Bloomberg School of Public Health, October 11, 2006

[16]   Sharp, Gene. *Waging Nonviolent Struggle: 20th Century Practice And 21st Century Potential.* Boston: Porter Sargent Publishers Inc., 2005.

[17]   Gandhi, M.K. Dear, John, ed. *Mohandas Gandhi. Essential Writings.* New York: Orbis, 2005.

[18]   Roberts, Elizabeth and Amidon, Elias. *Life Prayers From Around the World.* San Francisco: Harper, 1996.

[19]   ibid.

Illusion 7: The military will take good care of our soldiers

[1]   Zoroya, Gregg. "Troops Waiting for Medical Care." *USA Today*, June 5, 2007

[2]   Kennedy, Kelly. "More Help Sought for Suicidal Veterans." *Army Times*, May 7, 2007

[3]   Nadelson, Theodore. Trained to Kill: Soldiers at War. The Johns Hopkins University Press, 2005.

[4]   Lowe, Christian. "Mental Illness Plagues Current Vets." Military.Com, March 13, 2007

[5]   Kennedy, Kelly. "Lawmakers Urge VA to Take 'Bold Action.'" *Army Times*, May 21, 2007

[6]   Zoroya, Gregg. "Staffing at Vet Centers Lagging." *USA Today*, April 20, 2007

[7]   "Therapists Hard to Get for Soldiers." Associated Press dispatch, June 11, 2007

[8]   Putrich, Gayle S. "Your Guide to Anthrax Shots." *Army Times*, December 25, 2006

173

[9]   Uhl, Michael and Ensign, Tod. *GI Guinea Pigs: How the Pentagon Exposed Our Troops to Dangers More Deadly Than War.* Playboy Press, 1980.
[10]   York, Michelle. "The Army Makes Peace With a Former Medic." *The New York Times,* July 15, 2007
[11]   Maze, Rich. "Senate Panel Oks $1B in Vets' Benefits." *Army Times,* July 9, 2007

Illusion 8: War boosts the economy for all Americans
[1]   Leonhardt, David. "What $1.2 Trillion Can Buy." *The New York Times,* 12 Jan. 2007.
[2]   Henderson, Errol. "Military Spending and Poverty." T*he Journal of Politics* 60 (1998).
[3]   Abell, John. "Military Spending and Income Inequality." *Journal of Peace Research,* 31(1994).
[4]   "Historical Poverty Tables." U.S. Census Bureau: Poverty. 2006. Accessed: 29 Jun. 2007. <http://www.census.gov/hhes/www/poverty/histpov/hstpov21.html>
[5]   "Poverty: 2005 Highlights." U.S. Census Bureau: Poverty. 2006. Accessed: 29 Jun. 2007. <http://www.census.gov/hhes/www/poverty/poverty05/pov05hi.html>
[6]   MacAskill, Ewen. "Bush Slashes Aid to Poor to Boost Iraq War Chest." *The Guardian Unlimited Media* [Washington] 6 Feb. 2007. Accessed: 15 Jun. 2007. < http://www.guardian.co.uk/frontpage/story/0,,2006815,00.html >.
[7]   "Medicare Proposals in the President's 2007 Budget." National Committee to Preserve Social Security and Medicare. Accessed: 4 Jul. 2007.
[8]   ibid.
[9]   Reid, Harry. "Costs of War Underscore Need to Change Course in Iraq." US Fed News Service, Including US State News 08 May 2007: Proquest. Harold Washington Library. 15 Jun. 2007
[10]   ibid.
[11]   Ehrenreich, Barbara. "Bush's Bloat." *The Progressive* 70 (2006): 14-15.
[12]   "Cost: Paying the Price." *Mother Jones,* Apr/May 2007: 62-63.
[13]   "The War in Iraq Costs." National Priorities Project. Accessed August, 2007. <http://costofwar.com>

Illusion 9: We always win
[1]   Cumings, B. "On the strategy and morality of American nuclear policy in Korea, 1950 to the present." *Social Science Japan Journal* 1:57-70 (1998). Oxford University Press, 1998.
[2]   Panja, Tariq. Kissinger: Iraq Military Win Impossible. November 20, 2006. <http://www.washingtonpost.com/wp-dyn/content/article/2006/11/19/AR2006111900287_pf.html>
[3]   United Nations News Centre. Decrying violence in Iraq, UN envoy urges national dialogue, international support. November 25, 2006.
[4]   Lorentz, Al. Why We Cannot Win. LewRockwell.com, September 20, 2004. <http://www.lewrockwell.com/orig5/lorentz1.html>
[5]   Baldor, Lolita C. "Desertion rate leaps in Army." Associated Press, November 17, 2007.
[6]   Raum, Tom. U.S. Involvement in Iraq Longer Than WWII. CBS News, November 26, 2006. <http://www.cbsnews.com/stories/2006/11/26/ap/politics/mainD8LKO10O0.shtml>

Compassion
[1]   Hampson, Rick. "Effects of Iraq war vary dramatically in USA". *USA Today*, March 16, 2006.

2   "Civilians Without Protection: The ever-worsening humanitarian crisis in Iraq,"
      International Committee of the Red Cross, April 11, 2007.
3   Ted Koppel, ABC, January 17, 1991; Tom Brokaw, NBC, January 29, 1991.
4   President George W. Bush, March 17, 2003.

Illusion 10: Suffering is minimized in today's wars
1   Arnove, Anthony (Editor). *Iraq Under Siege: The Deadly Impact of Sanctions and
      War.* South End Press, 2002.
2   "Iraq Water Treatment Vulnerabilities," U.S. Defense Intelligence Agency. January
      22, 1991. <http://www.gulflink.osd.mil/declassdocs/dia/19950901/950901_
      511rept_91.html>
3   "Situation Analysis of Children and Women in Iraq - 1997." Unicef, April 1998.
4   "Iraq's Public Health Services Severely Strained, Group Says." New York Times,
      April 18, 2007 <http://www.nytimes.com/2007/04/18/world/middleeast/
      18health.html>
5   Galbraith, Peter. "The Surge." *New York Review of Books,* March 15, 2007.

Illusion 11: Our modern military warfare only kills the 'bad guys'
1   Jenkins, Simon. "Bombs That Turn our Leaders into Butchers." *The Times* (January
      17, 2001) <http://www.casi.org.uk/discuss/2001/msg00050.html>
2   Engelhardt, Tom. "Carnage from the Air and the Washington Consensus."
      TomDispatch.com (July 9, 2007) <http://www.tomdispatch.com/post/174817>
3   Herold, Marc. "War as an Edsel: The Marketing and Consumption of Modern
      American Wars" (Durham: keynote address at conference on "Teaching Peace," Oyster
      River High School, April 9, 2005). <http://pubpages.unh.edu/~mwherold>. See also
      Herman, Edward S. " 'They Kill Reporters, Don't They?' – Yes, as Part of a System
      of Information Control That Will Allow the Mass Killing of Civilians." *Z Magazine*
      18, 1 (January 2005). <http://zmagsite.zmag.org/Jan2005/herman0105.html>
4   Herold, Marc. "Truth about Afghan Civilian Casualties Comes Only through American
      Lenses for the U.S. Corporate Media [our modern-day Didymus]," in Peter Phillips
      and Project Censored [eds], *Censored 2003: the Year's Top 25 Stories* [New York:
      Seven Seas Publishing, 2002], pp. 265-294.
5   Zunes, Stephen. "Operation Enduring Freedom: A Retrospective." *Foreign Policy in
      Focus* (October 25, 2006) <http://www.fpif.org/fpiftxt/3616> This questions the
      notion that the U.S. war on Afghanistan was legal, moral, and a necessary response to
      protect American national security.
6   Hallion, Richard P. "Precision Guided Munitions and the New Era of Warfare"
      [Fairburn, Australia: Air Power Studies Center Working Paper #53, 1995] <http://
      www.fas.org/man/dod-101/sys/smart/docs/paper53.htm> This provides a marvelous
      history and analysis of the development of precision guided munitions.
7   Clemens, Walter C., Jr. and Singer, David J. "The Human Cost of War," *Scientific
      American* 282, 6 [June 2000]: 56-7. The breakdown for civilian and military casualties
      by nation during World War II. <http://ww2bodycount.netfirms.com>
8   Rhodes, Robert. "Man-made Death: A Neglected Mortality," JAMA Vol. 260, No.5
      (August 5, 1988): 686
9   Copeland, Robin M. "Effect of Type and Transfer of Conventional Weapons on
      Civilian Injuries: Retrospective Analysis of Prospective Data from Red Cross Hospitals,"
      British Medical Journal 319, issue 7207 [August 14, 1999]: 410-413. This provides
      a rare study which explores the link between different weapons used in modern wars
      and their potential to injure civilians, using case data for a Kabul hospital [1991-98].
10   Gannon, K. "Kandahar Road Traces Pashtun Heartland." A.P. [January 12, 2002,
      12:43 PM ET]. See also "Over 6,000 Killed, Taliban Still Prepared to Fight."

Frontier Post [November 28, 2001]; "10,000 Taliban Soldiers Killed in US raids." Agence France-Presse [December 7, 2001 at 12:07 IST]; Penketh, Anne. "Opposition Admits to Massacre of 520 Soldiers." November 16, 2001]; "Refugees Tell of Atrocities in Afghanistan." *The Star* [November 18, 2001].

[11] Hooglund, Eric. "The Other Face of War." *Middle East Report* no. 171 [July-August 1991]: 3-7, 10-12.

[12] Strada, Gino. *Green Parrots: A War Surgeon's Diary* (Charta, 2005). See also Herold, Marc. "Steel Rain: An Analysis of Cluster Bomb Usage by the US in Four Recent Campaigns." *www.cursor.org* (June 16, 2003) < http://www.cursor.org/stories/steelrain.html>

[13] Herold, Marc. "Above the Law and Below Morality: Data on 11 Weeks of U.S. Cluster-Bombing of Afghanistan." *www.cursor* (February 1, 2002) at http://www.cursor.org/stories/abovethelaw.htm

[14] The point has been made in conjunction with the [questionable] figures adduced by Arkin for the Kosovo air war, that *only* 500 civilians were killed in 78 days of NATO bombing, making it incomparably 'cleaner' than Allied bombing of Germany during World War II or "the horrors of Vietnam.". This argument fails to recognize that: [1] the Kosovo air campaign involved a low bombing intensity in terms of sorties per day; and [2] the relevant variable is some measure of civilians killed in relation to such bombing intensity. Some prefer to speculate that "in post-modern war, it may be possible to achieve victory while largely sparing civilians" [see Mike Moore, "A New Editor," *Bulletin of the Atomic Scientists* 56, 3 [May/June 2000]: 2-3]. Regarding civilian casualties in Kosovo, Fred Kaplan mentions the much more realistic figure of 1'200 [see Fred Kaplan, "Bombs Killing More Civilians than Expected," *Boston Globe* [May 30, 1999]: A33].

[15] Associated Press. "One Month In: How Three Different Wars Were Similar." *St. Petersburg Times* [November 4, 2001] <http://www.sptimes.com/News/110401/Worldandnation/One_month_in__How_ thr.shtml>

[16] Ingalls, James. "Smart Bombs over Iraq." *Z Magazine* [April 2003]: 9 <http://zmagsite.zmag.org/Apr2003/ingalls0403.html>

[17] Budiansky, Stephen. "How U.S Stretched the Limits of Air Power." *Washington Post* [December 23, 2001].

[18] Loeb, Vernon. "Bursts of Brilliance. How a String of Discoveries by Unheralded Engineers and Airmen Helped Bring America to the Pinnacle of Modern Military Power." *Washington Post* [December 15, 2002]. This provides a fascinating description of the development of precision bombs.

[19] Friedrich, Jorg. *Der Brand. Deutschland im Bombenkrieg 1940-1945* (Munich: Propylaen Verlag, 2002).

[20] Coffey, John W. "The Afghan Slaughter," *This World* 16 [1987]: 11-123. This explores the use of Soviet military force against Afghan civilians. Invariably, comparison with the Soviet air campaign in Afghanistan during the 1980s gets posed. Whereas the Soviet campaign in Afghanistan was clearly characterized by widespread *indiscriminate* killing of civilians reminiscent of strategic bombing, the initial U.S air campaign employing *more focused* bombing nonetheless resulted in significant civilian casualties, well above 3,000.

[21] Kiernan, Ben. " 'Collateral Damage' Means Real People." *The Bangkok Post* [October 20, 2002] <http://www.yale.edu/gsp/publications/collateral_damage.html> This explores the civilian casualties in Cambodia caused by U.S. bombing.

[22] Isaac, Jeffrey C. "Civilian Casualties in Afghanistan: the Limits of Marc Herold's 'Comprehensive Accounting'," *OpenDemocracy* [March 14, 2002] <http://www.opendemocracy.net/forum/document_details. asp?CatID=98&DocID=1143> This strange critique of my work states "why the US has bombed these areas is simply

because that is where the targeted facilities are located. But Herold strangely chooses to ignore this possibility."

23 Goodrich, Peter Spang. "The Surgical Precision Myth: After the Bomb Explodes — (CCDP) Cumulative Collateral Damage Probability." [Providence, R.I.: unpublished manuscript, Department of Management, Providence College, April 2003].

24 Wall, Robert. "Targeting, Weapon Supply Encumber Air Campaign." *Aviation Week & Space Technology* [October 22, 2001].

25 On the ground today soldiers are much more likely than their predecessors to actually fire their weapons. Soldiers' firing rates went from 25% in World War II, to 55% in Korea, and up to 90% in Vietnam. The Department of Defense has intentionally trained soldiers to fight reflexively rather than reflectively, which short-circuits all moral equivocation see Brad Knickerbocker, "In Era of High-Tech Warfare, 'Friendly-Fire' Risk Grows," *Christian Science Monitor* [January 14, 2003].

26 By impact death I mean death caused at the moment of explosion of the bomb or missile. This seriously underestimates the actual number of deaths as it omits all those injured who later die. My estimates indicate that for every impact death about two persons were injured.

27 Epstein, Jack. "U.S. Under Fire for Use of Cluster Bombs in Iraq. Pentagon Plays Down Dangers to Civilians," *San Francisco Chronicle* [May 15, 2003].

28 Goldenburg, Suzanne. "Long After the Air Raids, Bomblets Bring More Death." *The Guardian* [January 28, 2002]. <http://www.guardian.co.uk/afghanistan/story/0,1284,640486,00.html>

29 Gall, Carlotta. "Shattered Afghan Families Demand U.S Compensation." *The New York Times* [April 8, 2002].

30 See the website devoted to Carlos Marighela who "died for Brazil." <http://www.carlos.marighella.nom.br>

31 A difficulty exists here insofar as the U.S. military tries to minimize combat deaths and classifies some combat deaths as accidents. See Harring, Brian. "US Military Report: The High Death Rates Exposed." *TBRNews.org* (updated June 16, 2005). <http://www.tbrnews.org/Archives/a1669.htm> This questions the accuracy of officially reported U.S. military deaths.

32 Clemens, Walter C., Jr. and Singer, David J. "The Human Cost of War," *Scientific American* 282, 6 (June 2000): 56-7. See also Eckhardt, William. "Civilian Deaths in Wartime," *Bulletin of Peace Proposals* (Great Britain) 20, 1 (1989). 89-98. This analyzes the number and causes of civilian deaths in wartime during the period 1700-1987; Herold, Marc. "Urban Dimensions of the Punishment of Afghanistan by US Bombs." In Stephen Graham (ed), *Cities, War, and Terrorism. Towards an Urban Geopolitics* (Oxford: Blackwell Publishing, 2004), Table 17.2 on p. 316. Here I document the rising trend in civilian casualties from Vietnam to Iraq.

33 "Suicide car bombs vs. 'Precision' bombs," *Frontline.India's National Magazine* 23, 19 (September 23 – October 06, 2006). <http://www.hinduonnet.com/fline/fl2319/stories/20061006001205600.htm>

34 Herold, Marc. "Spinning out of Control. The U.S. Military's Virtual Reality about a Deadly Day in May (2006)." *Cursor.org* (May 30, 2006). <http://cursor.org/stories/grabnews.html>

35 "US Rejects Italy's Call to Withdraw from Afghanistan." Agence France Presse (July 26, 2007).

36 Harrison, David. "Britain Losing 'Hearts and Minds' in Afghanistan." *Sunday Telegraph* (July 22, 2007) and Adam Holloway, "What the Government Won't Tell: We are Losing Afghan Hearts," *Telegraph* (April 8, 2007).

[37] "Six Questions for Michael Scheuer on National Security." *Harper's Magazine* (August 2006). <http://www.harpers.org/archive/2006/08/sb-seven-michael-scheuer-1156277744>

[38] Herold, Marc. *Afganistan como un Espacio Vacio* (Madrid: Ediciones Akal, 2007). See also Margolis, Eric. "America's Ace. Without the Might of the U.S. Air Force, the Battle Would be Lost." *Edmonton Sun* (July 29, 2007). <http://www.edmontonsun.com/Comment/2007/07/29/4377094-sun.html>

Illusion 12: 'Collateral damage' is an impersonal by-product of war

[1] "Walk in Their Shoes." CodePINK <http://www.codepink4peace.org/article.php?list=type&type=176>

Illusion 13: War is temporary

[1] Scherrer, Christian. "DU and the Liberation of Iraq: A report from Hiroshima." ZNet, April 13, 2003 <http://www.zmag.org/content/showarticle.cfm?SectionID=15&ItemID=3453>.

[2] "Radioactive War." CounterPunch, February 5, 2001 <http://www.counterpunch.org/du.html>.

[3] Peterson, Scott. "Remains of Toxic Bullets Litter Iraq." *Christian Science Monitor*, May 15, 2003.

[4] Caldicott, Helen. *Nuclear Power is not the Answer.* The New Press, 2006.

[5] Baverstock, K., Motherstill, C. and Thorne, M. "Radiological toxicity of DU. Repressed WHO Document, 2001 <http://www.mindfully.org/Nucs/DU-Radiological-Toxicity-WHO5nov01.htm>.

[6] Gardner, Phil. "Casualties increase from use of depleted uranium." World Socialist Web Site, 8 September 1999 <http://www.wsws.org/articles/1999/sep1999/gulf-s08.shtml>.

[6] O'Kane, Maggie. "Attack on Iraq." *The Guardian* (UK), December 21, 1998 <http://nucnews.net/2000/du/98du/981221.htm>.

[7] Tucker Jr., James P. "DU Death Toll Tops 11,000." American Free Press, March 26, 2005 <http://www.americanfreepress.net/html/du_death_toll.html>.

[8] "Depleted uranium casts shadow over peace in Iraq." *New Scientist.* 15 April 2003 <http://www.newscientist.com/article/dn3627.html>.

[10] Schröder et al. *Radiation Protection Dosimetry*, vol. 103, p 211.

[11] Watson, Paul Joseph. "Israelis Rain Down Deadly DU On Lebanese Civilians." Prison Planet.com, July 28 2006.

[12] "Doctor's Gulf War Studies Link Cancer to Depleted Uranium." *The New York Times*, January 29, 2001.

[13] Flanders, L. "Mal de Guerre." *The Nation*, March 7, 1994.

[14] Bollyn, C. "DU Syndrome Stricken Vets Denied Care." American Free Press, August 20, 2004.

[15] Boyle, Francis. *Biowarfare and Terrorism.* Clarity Press, 2005.

[16] Johnson, Chalmers. *The Sorrows of Empire: Militarism, Secrecy, and the End of the Republic* (American Empire Project). Metropolitan Books, 2004,

Altruism

[1] "World View of US Role Goes From Bad to Worse." BBC World Service poll. January 23, 2007.

[2] "Global Unease With Major World Powers." Pew Global Attitudes Survey. 06/27/07.

Illusion 14: America's relationship with Israel promotes stability in the Middle East.

1   Kolko, Gabriel. "Israel's Last Chance." AntiWar.com, 3/17/2007, pp. 1-2.

2   Mearsheimer, John and Walt, Stephen. "The Israel Lobby," *The London Review of Books*, March 23, 2006, passim.

3   Boyle, Francis A. "Violations of International Law," *Middle East International*, September 3, 1982, 11.

4   President Bush Commends Israeli Prime Minister Sharon's Plan. April, 2004. <http://www.whitehouse.gov/news/releases/2004/04/20040414-4.html>.

5   Halper, Jeff. "The Livni-Rice Plan: Towards a Just Peace or Apartheid ?," Israel Committee Against House Demolitions, 2 May, 2007, pp. 1-5.

6   Akbarzadeh, Shahram and Connor, Kylie. "The Organization of the Islamic Conference: Sharing an Illusion," *Middle East Policy*, Vol. XII, No. 2. Summer, 2005, 85.

7   ibid., 86-9.

Illusion 15: Developing countries ultimately benefit from our wars for democracy

1   Montague, Dena and Berrigan, Frida. "The Business of War in the Democratic Republic of Congo: Who Benefits?" Dollars and Sense: Arms Trade Resource Center July/August 2001 <http://www.worldpolicy.org/projects/arms/news/dollarsandsense.html>.

2   "New Report Documents U.S. Role in Fueling African Conflicts," Arms Trade Resource Center, January 24, 2000 <http://www.worldpolicy.org/projects/arms/updates/pressrel2.htm>. See also Snow, Keith Harmon and Barouski, David. "Behind the Numbers: Untold Suffering in the Congo." Znet, March 1, 2006; "US in Africa: Partnership or Pillage?" MADRE, Spring 2000 <http://www.madre.org/articles/afr/usinafrica.html>.

3   "Congo: Nearly 4 Million Dead in 6 Year Conflict" International Rescue Committee<http://www.theirc.org/where/democratic_republic_of_congo_38_million_dead_in_6_year_conflict.html>.Independent journalists note that the 4 million dead is a low figure, particularly seeing that the number does not include the deaths from the 1996 Rwandan invasion. See Barouski, David and Snow, Keith Harmon. "Behind the Numbers Untold Suffering in the Congo." zmag.org March 1, 2006 <http://www.zmag.org/content/showarticle.cfm?SectionID=2&ItemID=9832>

4   DRC Mortality Survey 2004. Washington Presentation: Power Point Presentation. Provided to Friends of the Congo by the International Rescue Committee

5   The Lancet Publishes IRC Mortality Study from DR Congo; 3.9 Million Have Died: 38,000 Die per Month. International Rescue Committee, January 2006 <http://www.theirc.org/news/page-27819067.html>

6   <http://friendsofthecongo.org/reports/index.php>.

7   Final Report of the Panel of Experts on the Illegal Exploitation of Natural Resources and Other Forms of Wealth of Democratic Republic of Congo (S/2002/1146)

8   Robert Block, "U.S. Firms Seek Deals in Central Africa," *Wall Street Journal*, 14 October 1997.

9   "Bush's Choice for Energy Secretary One of 'Top Five' Polluters," Environmentalists Against War, January 19, 2005 <http://www.envirosagainstwar.org/know/read.php?itemid=2274>

Illusion 16: The environmental consequences of war are insignificant

1   Sherwood, J. "The pulse of the planet." Canada & the World Backgrounder, October 1995, 61(2)4.

2   Lambroschini, A. Soviet nuclear legacy still poisons Kazakhstan, Agence France-Presse, 2007.

3   War on the Environment. *Ecologist*. 33(4) 44. May, 2003,

[4] Sandel, M. J. *Public philosophy: Essays on morality in politics.* Cambridge MA: Harvard University Press, 2005.

[5] Eisler, P. "Pollution cleanups pit Pentagon against regulators." *USA Today*, 10/14/04 <http://www.usatoday.com/news/nation/2004-10-14-cover-pollution_x.htm>.

[6] Stranahan, S. Q. "Target practice." *Mother Jones*, Jul/Aug2001. 26(4) 21.

[7] Tully, J. Vietnam: war and the environment, Green Left, 1993. <http://www.greenleft.org.au/1993/106/5903>

[8] Hastings, T. H. *Ecology of war & peace: Counting costs of conflict.* Lanham MD: University Press of America, 2000. See also Jarrett, R. "The environment: Collateral victim and tool of war." *Bioscience*, September 2003. 53(9)880-882.

[9] Project Censored. U.S. military's war on the earth. 2004. <http://www.projectcensored.org/Publications/2004/15.html> To get more information contact the Military Toxics Project, P.O. Box 558, Lewiston, ME 04243; call 207-783-5091; www.miltoxproj.org or e-mail steve@miltoxproj.org . Seth Shulman's early 1990s book, "The Threat At Home: Confronting the Toxic Legacy of the U.S. Military," also contains information about the Pentagon's "War on the Earth" within the US's borders.

[10] "Pentagon Pollution." USA Today, 2007. <http://www.usatoday.com/news/graphics/pentagon_pollution/flash.htm>

[11] Gluckman, R.; Hartmann, B. & Shariatmadar, A. "Pro-whose-life?" *Women's Review of Books*, September 2004. 21(12, 12-13.

[12] Ackerman, P., & Karatnycky, A. How freedom is won: From civic resistance to durable democracy. NYC: Freedom House, 2005 <http://www.freedomhouse.org/uploads/special_report/29.pdf>

[13] Hastings, op. cit. See also Burton, C. Book review. *Peace & Change*. July 2003. 28(3)455-457.

Realism

[1] Pancirollus, Guido. "The History of Many memorable Things lost, Which were in Use among the Ancients, and an Account of many excellent Things found, now in Use among the Moderns, both Natural and Artificial." London: Little-Britain, Stationers-hall, 1715.

[2] Barash, David P. and Webel, Charles P. *Peace and Conflict Studies.* Sage Publications, 2002.

[3] Angell, Norman. *Europe's Optical Illusion.* London, 1909.

[4] Barash and Webel, op. cit.

[5] Fry, Douglas P. *Beyond Wars: The Human Potential for Peace.* Oxford University Press, 2007.

[6] Ember, C. and Ember, M. "Warfare, aggression, and resource problems: cross-cultural codes." Behavioral Science Research 26, 1992. See also Ember, C. and Ember, M. "War, socialization, and interpersonal violence: A cross-cultural study." *Journal of Conflict Resolution* 38, 1994; Otterbein, Keith (ed). *Feuding and Warfare: Selected Works of Keith F. Otterbein.* Gordon & Breach, 1994; Otterbein, Keith. "A history of research on warfare in anthropology." *American Anthropologist* 101, 1999.

[7] Wright, Quincy. *A Study of War.* University of Chicago Press, 1942.

Illusion 17: I personally have no better options than the military.

[1] Headquarters United States Army Recruiting Command. Training School Recruiting Program Handbook (p1). USAREC Pamphlet 350-13. April 2002.

[2] ibid., p. 3.

[3] Allison, Aimee and Solnit, David. *Army of None: Strategies to Counter Military Recruitment. End War, and Build a Better World.* Seven Stories Press (p9), 2007.

[4] US Army <http://www.goarmy.com/life/living_the_army_values.jsp? fl=false>.

5   Allison, Aimee and Solnit, David, op. cit.

6   ibid.

7   Harris Interactive Case Studies: Client United States Department of Defense <http://www.harrisinteractive.com/services/government_casestudy.asp>.

8   *Washington Post*: "Army Guard Refilling Its Ranks" <http//www.washingtonpost.com/wp-dyn/content/article/2006/03/11/AR2006031101342_pf.html>.

9   Butler, Smedley Major General. *War Is a Racket*. Round Table Press, 1935.

10 US Army <http://www.army.mil/armybtkc/gov/values.htm>.

11 King Jr., Dr. Martin Luther. A Call to Conscience: The Landmark Speeches of Dr. Martin Luther King, Jr. "Beyond Vietnam" Address delivered at Riverside Church NY. 4 April 1967.

12 Mangum, Stephen L. and Ball, David E. "Military Service and Post-Service Labor Market Outcomes." Center for Human Resource Research, The Ohio State University, 1984.

13 Barley, S. R. "Military Downsizing and the Career Prospects of Youth." Annals of the American Academy of Social and Political Sciences (p559), 1998.

14 Allison, Aimee and Solnit, David, op. cit.

15 Headquarters United States Army Recruiting Command. Training School Recruiting Program Handbook (7). USAREC Pamphlet 350-13. April 2002.

16 ibid.

17 Brown, Jenny "Opposition to Military Recruitment Crimps Bush Plan for Endless War" <http://www.afn.org/~iguana/archives/2005_07/20050701.html> July/August 2005.

18 Allen, Terry "GI Bill Fails Vets," April 2007 <http://www.inthesetimes.com/article/3134/gi_bill_fails_vets/>.

19 Counter-Recruitment.Org <http://www.counter-recruitment.org>. See also American Friends Service Committee <http://afsc.org/youthmil>.

20 America's Job Bank (guides to finding a job). <www.ajb.org>. See also Job Corps (job training and support from US Department of Labor for low income youth). <www.jobcorps.doleta.gov>; Employment & Training / US Dept of Labor. <www.doleta.gov>; Inroads Home (leadership training and internships for minority youth). <www.inroads.org>; Idealist Social Action (jobs and volunteer opportunities that include education and travel). <www.idealist.org>; Social Service job opportunities. <www.socialservice.com>, <www.appleseednetworkorg>, Americorps, VISTA (Combines jobs, travel, community service and training with ways to earn money for college and relief from student loans). <www.americorps.org>, <www.nationalservices.org>.

21 Federal Student Aid (FAFSA) and Government money <www.ed.gov/thinkcollege>.

22 The Student Guide to Financial Aid <www.studentaid.ed.gov>.

23 <www.freescholarshipguide.com>, <www.icanaffordcollege.com>, <www.collegeispossible.org>, <www.college411.org>, <www.get-recruited.com>.

24 GI Rights Hotline / Central Committee for Conscientious Objectors <http://www.girights.org>.

25 National Public Radio: National Guard struggles to recruit <http://www.npr.org/templates/story/story.php?storyId=5176841>.

26 U.S. Navy Delayed Entry Program (DEP) <http://www.cnrc.navy.mil/DEP/index.htm>.

27 U.S. Military <http://usmilitary.about.com/cs/joiningup/a/dep.htm>.

28 Knappenberger, Evan M. "Rampant Militarism (A Personal Analysis)" Iraq Veterans Against the War <http://www.ivaw.org >. October 2007.

Conclusion

[1] Stockholm International Peace Research Institute (SIPRI) Yearbook 2006. <http://yearbook2006.sipri.org/chap8>. See also "World Wide Military Expenditures" <http://www.globalsecurity.org/military/world/spending.htm>; "U.S. Military Spending vs. the World," Center for Arms Control and Non-Proliferation, February 5, 2007; Conventional Arms Transfers to Developing Nations, 1998-2005," CRS Report for Congress, October 23, 2006; Berrigan, Frida and Hartung, William D., with Leslie Heffel. "U.S. Weapons at War 2005: Promoting Freedom or Fueling Conflict?" June 2005; "The G8: Global Arms Exporters: Failing to prevent irresponsible arms transfers" Amnesty International, IANSA, Oxfam International, June 2005.

[2] Blum, William. *Rogue State: A Guide to the World's Only Superpower.* Common Courage Press, 2000.

[3] Ricks, Thomas. *Fiasco: The American Military Adventure in Iraq.* Penguin Books, 2006.

[4] Pape, Robert A. "Suicide Terrorism and Democracy: What We've Learned Since 9/11." Cato Institute, September 8, 2006. See also Bueno de Mesquita, Bruce and Downs, George W. "Why Gun-Barrel Democracy Doesn't Work." The Hoover Digest, January 23, 2006; Eland, Ivan. "Does U.S. Intervention Overseas Breed Terrorism? The Historical Record. Cato Institute, December 17, 1998; Bergen, Peter and Cruickshank, Paul. "The Iraq Effect: War Has Increased Terrorism Sevenfold Worldwide." Mother Jones, March 1, 2007; "Year Four: Simply the worst," Press release 15: Iraq Body Count March 18th 2007; "The Terrorism Index." Foreign Policy & The Center For American Progress, July/August 2006.

[5] "US Position on International Treaties," Updated July, 2003. <http://www.globalpolicy.org/empire/tables/treaties.htm>. See also "Convention on the Rights of the Child," UNICEF. <http://www.unicef.org/crc/index_30229.html>; "U.S. Opposes Right to Food at World Summit," Peter Rosset, Food First, June 30, 2002; Human Rights Watch World Report 2006 <www.hrw.org>; United Nations Population Fund, January 2006; "U.S. ousted from U.N. Human Rights Commission." CNN.com, May 3, 2001; "UN approves Human Rights Council over US opposition," University of Pittsburgh School of Law, March 15, 2006; "Global Governance Initiative: Annual Report 2006." <http://www.weforum.org/pdf/Initiatives/GGI_Report06.pdf>; "UN Finance." Global Policy Forum, accessed February 2007. <http://www.globalpolicy.org/finance>.

[6] Bagdikian, Ben. *The New Media Monopoly.* Beacon Press, 2004. See also "Big Six U.S. TV Companies." TVNewsday, April 21, 2006; "And then there were eight: 25 years of media mergers, from GE-NBC to Google-YouTube," *Mother Jones*, March 2007.

[7] United Nations: Human Development Report 2005 <http://hdr.undp.org/reports/global/2005/pdf/HDR05_chapter_2.pdf>. See also "Historical Income Tables - Income Equality," U.S. Census Bureau, May 2004; United Nations Human Development Report 2005; World Bank, "World Development Report 2006"; "The Income Gap." US News & World Report, January 22, 2007; "Income Gap Is Widening, Data Shows." New York Times, March 29, 2007; "The Bush Tax Cuts Enacted Through 2006: The Latest CTJ Data. June 22, 2006 <http://ctj.org/pdf/gwbdata.pdf>; Friedman, Joel. "The Decline of Corporate Income Tax Revenues." Center on Budget and Policy Priorities, October 24, 2003; World Institute for Development Economics Research of the United Nations University (UNU-WIDER), "The World Distribution of Household Wealth," December 5, 2006; "Corporate Tax Dodgers: The Decline in U.S. Corporate Taxes and the Rise in Offshore Tax Haven Abuses," Center for Corporate Policy, accessed September 2007.

[8]   "Americans on Foreign Aid and World Hunger: A Study of U.S. Public Attitudes, Program on International Policy Attitudes," 2001 and 2006. See also "Official Development Assistance increases further - but 2006 targets still a challenge." Organisation for Economic Co-operation and Development, 11/04/2005; Hirvonen, Pekka. "Stingy Samaritans: Why Recent Increases in Development Aid Fail to Help the Poor." Global Policy Forum, August 2005; "Foreign Aid: An Introductory Overview of U.S. Programs and Policy," Congressional Research Service, The Library of Congress, January 19, 2005; "Paying the Price: Why rich countries must invest now in a war on poverty," Oxfam International 2005; Adelman, Carol. "The Index of Global Philanthropy 2006." Center for Global Prosperity; Radelet, Steven. "Think Again: U.S. Foreign Aid." Center for Global Development, February 2005; "International comparisons of charitable giving." Charities Aid Foundation, November 2006.

[9]   "Human Development Report 2005: A Compendium of Inequality." <http://hdr.undp.org/reports/global/2005>. See also Stiglitz, Joseph. "It Takes More than Free Trade to End Poverty." GlobalPolicy.org, February 3, 2006; "The economics of failure: The real cost of 'free' trade for poor countries," A Christian Aid briefing paper, June 2005; "The Damage Done: Aid, Death and Dogma." Christian Aid 2005; "Effects of Financial Globalization on Developing Countries," IMF Occasional Paper 220, 2003; "World Economy Giving Less to Poorest in Spite of Global Poverty," New Economics Foundation, January 23, 2006; Chua, Amy. World On Fire: How Exporting Free Market Democracy Breeds Ethnic Hatred and Global Instability. New York: Anchor Books, 2004

[10]   Thoreau, Henry David. "Civil Disobedience." <http://sunsite.berkeley.edu/Literature/Thoreau/CivilDisobedience.html>. See also Euben, J. Peter. "Critical Patriotism." <http://www.aaup.org/publications/Academe/2002/02so/02sojeu.htm>.

[11]   King, Martin Luther, Jr. "A Time to Break Silence." April 4th, 1967.

INDEX